ORTHO'S All About

Roofing
and Siding Basics

Meredith® Books
Des Moines, Iowa

Ortho® Books
An imprint of Meredith® Books

Ortho's All About Roofing and Siding
Editor: Larry Johnston
Contributing Editor: Martin Miller
Contributing Writer: Jeremy Powers
Art Director: Tom Wegner
Assistant Art Director: Harijs Priekulis
Copy Chief: Catherine Hamrick
Copy and Production Editor: Terri Fredrickson
Book Production Managers: Pam Kvitne,
    Marjorie J. Schenkelberg
Contributing Copy Editor: Steve Hallam
Technical Proofreader: Ray Kast
Contributing Proofreaders: Dan Degen, Debra Morris Smith,
    Sue Fetters
Indexer: Barbara L. Kline
Electronic Production Coordinator: Paula Forest
Editorial and Design Assistants: Kathleen Stevens,
    Karen Schirm

Additional Editorial Contributions from
    Art Rep Services
Director: Chip Nadeau
Designer: lk Design
Illustrator: Dave Brandon

Meredith® Books
Editor in Chief: James D. Blume
Design Director: Matt Strelecki
Managing Editor: Gregory H. Kayko
Executive Ortho Editor: Larry Erickson

Director, Retail Sales and Marketing: Terry Unsworth
Director, Sales, Special Markets: Rita McMullen
Director, Sales, Premiums: Michael A. Peterson
Director, Sales, Retail: Tom Wierzbicki
Director, Sales, Home & Garden Centers: Ray Wolf
Director, Book Marketing: Brad Elmitt
Director, Operations: George A. Susral
Director, Production: Douglas M. Johnston

Vice President, General Manager: Jamie L. Martin

Meredith Publishing Group
President, Publishing Group: Christopher M. Little
Vice President, Finance & Administration: Max Runciman

Meredith Corporation
Chairman and Chief Executive Officer: William T. Kerr
Chairman of the Executive Committee: E.T. Meredith III

Photographers
(Photographers credited may retain copyright ©
    to the listed photographs.)
L = Left, R = Right, C = Center, B = Bottom, T = Top
Alcoa Building Products, Inc.: 57B, 58T
Baldwin Photography: front cover
Laurie Black: 3T, 16, 56BR, 78T
Eldorado Stone Corporation: 79T
Hetherington Photography: 59
Hopkins Associates: 84T
Michael Jensen: 57T
Scott Little: 3C, 26
Metal Roofing Alliance: 50
Saïd Nuseibeh: 3B, 54
Kenneth Rice: 58C
Jamie Salomon: 4
Marvin Sloben, California Redwood Association: 56BL
Rick Taylor: 15

All of us at Ortho® Books are dedicated to providing you
with the information and ideas you need to enhance your
home and garden. We welcome your comments and
suggestions about this book. Write to us at:
    Meredith Corporation
    Ortho Books
    1716 Locust St.
    Des Moines, IA 50309–3023

If you would like more information on other Ortho
products, call 800-225-2883 or visit us at www.ortho.com

Note to the Readers: Due to differing conditions, tools,
and individual skills, Meredith Corporation assumes no
responsibility for any damages, injuries suffered, or losses
incurred as a result of following the information published
in this book. Before beginning any project, review the
instructions carefully, and if any doubts or questions remain,
consult local experts or authorities. Because codes and
regulations vary greatly, you always should check with
authorities to ensure that your project complies with all
applicable local codes and regulations. Always read and
observe all of the safety precautions provided by
manufacturers of any tools, equipment, or supplies,
and follow all accepted safety procedures.

ROOFING AND SIDING BASICS

Your home is probably your most valued possession in terms of money, pride, and comfort. Its shell—the roofing and siding—shields its structure and you from the elements.

Roofing and siding also contribute greatly to how your home looks. They should harmonize with each other and suit the style of your house and neighborhood. For lasting appearance and protection, roofing and siding require periodic inspection and maintenance.

The distinctive textures and rich appearance of many of today's roofing and siding materials give a home an expensive, custom look at reasonable cost. Today's roofing and siding materials last longer with less maintenance than those available just a few years ago.

Wooden and asphalt shingles once reigned as the roofing standards. Now, residential roofs are just as likely to be covered with metal or fiber-reinforced concrete shingles.

Whether you're remodeling or building new, this book tells you what you need to know about choosing, installing, and maintaining roofing and siding. This book will help you make decisions to protect your home and add to its curb appeal.

Roofing and siding establish your home's look and help define its style. Texture and line can highlight architectural features or bring interest to surfaces. A change in roofing or siding often alters a house's character.

This chapter provides guidelines for inspecting and evaluating your roofing and siding. It will help you determine whether they need repair or replacement. If you decide on replacement, this chapter will help you plan the job, estimate time and costs, remind you about codes and permits, and help you decide if you should hire a contractor. Subsequent chapters show you in detail how to do the work yourself and how to maintain and repair roofing and siding.

BEFORE YOU BEGIN

Roofing and siding jobs often require tearing off old shingles or siding. This is not complicated, but it is hard, dusty, dirty work. You'll have to load and haul a lot of debris, too (or pay someone else to do it).

Find out about your local landfill's policies regarding common building materials. Environmental safety concerns complicate removal of some products. During the 1950s, for example, fiber cement siding contained asbestos. Today the U.S. Environmental Protection Agency and most states regulate asbestos disposal.

If you suspect your home's siding contains asbestos, call a professional listed under Asbestos Abatement or Waste Disposal–Hazardous in the Yellow Pages.

When you remove roofing or siding from an older home, you may uncover structural members that need repair. That can affect the project's cost and timetable. Replacing the roof deck on a home could easily double a roofing job's time and cost. To avoid surprises, inspect the roof deck from the attic first. For siding, remove pieces along the bottom and at several other heights on one side or the back of your home to check the sheathing.

Whether you do it yourself or pay someone to do it, roofing and siding is tough on the greenery around your home's foundation. Even with the best of intentions, flowers will get stomped and shrubbery can be broken. Use old, light-colored sheets, thrown over the top of shrubs and pull them away from the house with rope tied to a stake to minimize damage.

TERMS

1. Chimney base flashing
2. Eaves
3. Fascia
4. Horizontal siding
5. Housewrap
6. Lookout
7. Rake
8. Ridge beam
9. Ridge shingles
10. Roof edge
11. Roof sheathing (boards)
12. Roof sheathing (plywood)

13. Roof truss
14. Shingle siding
15. Shingles
16. Soffit
17. Step flashing
18. Underlayment
19. Valley
20. Valley flashing
21. Vent flashing
22. Vertical panel siding
23. Wall sheathing
24. Wall stud

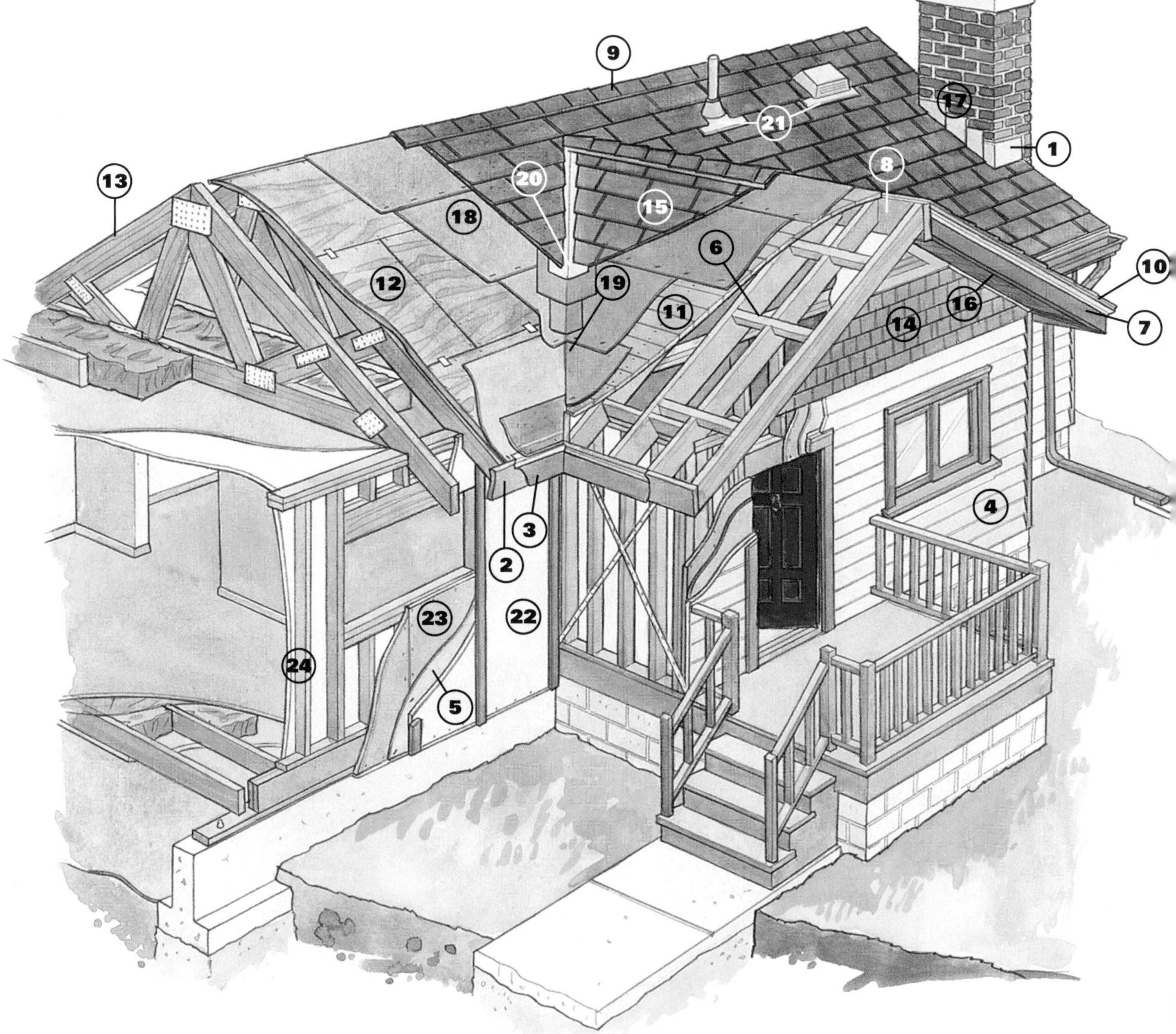

THE WELL-SEALED HOME

A number of elements work together to form a house's protective shell, as shown by the illustration. Even those items that don't show—such as the underlayment beneath the shingles and the vapor barrier under the siding—must overlap, from top to bottom.

Roofing and siding keep water out of the living spaces in your home as well as the insulating envelope created in the walls and ceiling. Wet insulation doesn't insulate. A well-insulated and well-ventilated attic also helps keep out the elements by reducing ice dams and condensation in winter and overheated attics in summer.

The correct application of roofing and siding requires careful attention to detail. New construction proceeds from the inside out, with each succeeding layer protecting the one beneath it. The illustration at right shows, for instance, that a drip cap over a window is installed before the overlapping siding. When remodeling, restore each piece to maintain the protection originally built into the house.

Before you begin any work—whether new construction, remodeling, or repairs—read and understand the general section on roofing and siding, as well as the section on your specific project. When you begin a roof or siding job, your house is open to the elements. Stopping to read what to do next could be costly if a storm blows in.

This book will show you how to install roofing and siding so that your house is properly protected.

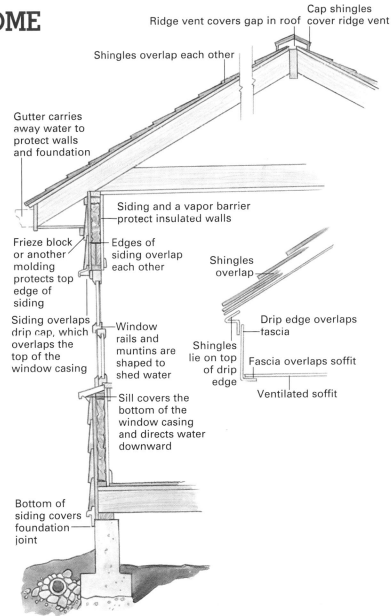

EXTERIOR STYLES

Roofing and siding are major contributors to your home's appearance. The roofing and siding should agree with the architectural style of the house. They should harmonize with each other, too. Also, consider any other structures on your property, such as a detached garage or shed. You may want to roof or side them to match the house for a unified look.

A roof with texture and depth will usually look richer and more substantial than one with a flat, plain surface. This accounts for the popularity of laminated composition shingles that give the dimension and shadow lines of wooden shakes or shingles. Many modern roofing materials replicate at reasonable cost the look of slate tiles or other expensive, hard-to-install materials. Just be careful that the roofing you select won't overwhelm the rest of the house.

Siding offers few color choices; you'll have to paint to have a custom color. Roofing colors may be limited, too. But when you have a choice, pick one that goes with your trim and siding. (See page 25 for more about this.)

Some people specify light-colored composition shingles to keep the house cool. But, this may not be entirely effective. Researchers at the U.S. Department of Energy Lawrence Berkeley National Laboratory found that even white composition shingles absorb most of the solar radiation that hits them. In one test, white fiberglass/asphalt shingles reached a surface temperature of 118 degrees Fahrenheit on a sunny, 55-degree day. The surface of clay terra-cotta tiles went to 112 degrees, and a coat of red acrylic paint peaked at 106 degrees. So, just pick a color you like and call it cool.

FINDING FAULTS

LOOKING FOR ROOF PROBLEMS

Don't wait for a problem to develop before you consider replacing your roof. Here the old saying "An ounce of prevention is worth a pound of cure" takes precedence over "If it isn't broken, don't fix it." Most roofs—even metal or stone ones—will eventually wear out. It's best to replace a roof before a problem forces you to.

A close inspection will probably identify most roof problems. First, stand back and look

Common roof problems include loose, torn, or missing shingles; bent flashing; cupped or curled shingles; popped nails; and places where granules have worn off. Check your roof after a rain; puddles show where problems are beginning.

HOW OLD IS YOUR ROOF?

Here's an easy way to determine the approximate age of a three-tab composition-shingle roof: Measure the width of the shingle slots.

The slots in new shingles measure ⅛ to 3⁄16 of an inch wide at about 70 degrees. If a regular wooden pencil fits in the slots, the shingles are about 10 years old and still have life in them. Slots that have grown to about ½ inch wide indicate that the shingles are near the end of their useful life and should be replaced soon. If the slots have widened to ¾ inch or more, the roof has exceeded its normal life and problems could occur at any time. Take your measurements in the morning before the sun has warmed the shingles.

The slots create the characteristic shingle tabs and allow for expansion. The slots widen over time because the edges, which aren't covered by mineral granules, deteriorate.

at your roof. Then go up on the roof with a screwdriver and stiff putty knife. (See safety guidelines, pages 10 through 13.)

ON ALL ROOFS, LOOK FOR:
■ Popped nails
■ Loose or missing flashing around vent pipes, chimneys, and wall junctions
■ Cracks or gaps in caulking material
■ Holes in the valley material (a valley is formed where one roof surface meets another)
■ Rot. Gently pry up the material at the valleys and eaves with a putty knife. At the eaves; you should be able to push in a screwdriver tip no more than a ½ an inch, preferably less

ON COMPOSITION SHINGLE ROOFS, LOOK FOR:
■ Areas where the granules have worn off
■ Missing shingle tabs
■ Badly cupped or curled shingles
■ Puddles during or immediately after a rain

ON WOOD SHAKE OR SHINGLE ROOFS, LOOK FOR:
■ Missing shingles
■ Warped shingles
■ Dark stains that could be a sign of rot

Next, go into the attic. Inspect the underside of the roof deck. Even if you haven't seen a leak in the living quarters, water could have leaked through the roof into the attic, causing rot or other problems. Look for telltale water stains. Poke suspicious spots with the screwdriver. Also look for matted or crusted insulation—signs that water has been dripping on it.

HOW TO FIND A ROOF LEAK

Leaks are difficult to find, even for professional roofers. Rarely does a drip or water spot in the ceiling indicate a leak directly above it in the roof. Water can trickle a considerable distance between the shingles and the roof deck, or inside the attic on the edge of a rafter, before it finally drops onto the attic side of the ceiling. The water can travel farther still before it finds a hole in the ceiling vapor barrier.

If a leak develops, carefully inspect the roof, as explained previously. Mark any holes you find with spray paint. Look for obstructions in valleys—they can dam water so it backs up under the shingles.

If you don't find anything obviously wrong

on the roof, go into the attic on a bright day. Darken the attic and look for light shining through a hole. Inspect around vent pipes, chimneys, and skylights—places where the roof deck has been cut and resealed. The sealing material or flashing is often the culprit.

If you still can't find the leak, start right above the spot in the ceiling and look for watermarks. Or follow the probable path of the water along the rafters or the underside of the roof deck. Assess how gravity would influence the water flow, and try to trace the leak upstream to its origin.

Finally, if nothing else works, flood suspected areas of the roof with a garden hose while someone in the attic watches for the drip. Begin watering below the point where you think the leak is. Slowly work your way up the roof slope.

Leaks can be difficult to find because water travels along rafters or on top of tar paper or plastic until it finds a place to come into the house. Try tracing the leak from inside the attic. Look for water stains on the rafters and roof decks.

LOOKING FOR SIDING PROBLEMS

Siding usually suffers fewer problems than roofing. More often, people change siding to give the house a new look or simply because the siding is old. After being repainted over flaking coats of paint a few times, siding begins to look shabby. This often occurs long before the siding fails to protect the home. Poke a screwdriver into the siding, window and door frames, and other areas to find soft, punky wood that is the first sign of rot.

HERE ARE SOME SIDING PROBLEMS TO LOOK FOR:
■ Extensive paint bubbling, cracking, or peeling; an insufficient vapor barrier or lack of insulation often causes this
■ Cracks in the exterior sheathing where water can get in
■ Warped trim or uncaulked openings around the doors and windows and at the corners of the building
■ Gaps where the siding meets any other surface, such as a chimney
■ Warped siding that's creating a bulge

Inspect siding for cracked or missing pieces, insect or bird damage, missing caulk, and gaps between pieces of siding. Warped siding or bubbled paint can indicate that moisture inside the home is passing through the walls due to an inadequate vapor barrier.

SAFETY, FIRST AND LAST

In any job, nothing is more important than safety for the people doing the work. Carelessness on the job and failure to take proper precautions invite trouble. Adequate safety equipment and adherence to safe working techniques help prevent injury.

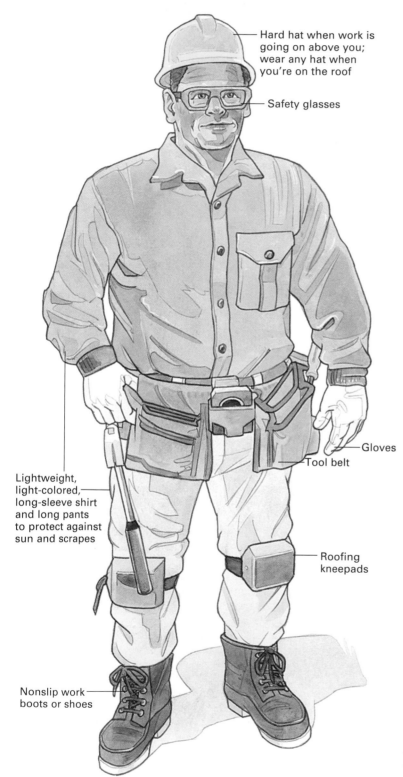

Hard hat when work is going on above you; wear any hat when you're on the roof

Safety glasses

Gloves

Tool belt

Lightweight, light-colored, long-sleeve shirt and long pants to protect against sun and scrapes

Roofing kneepads

Nonslip work boots or shoes

THE WORKER – MENTALLY

If you enjoy the feeling of accomplishment or the physical work that goes with home improvement projects, this is a good project to take on. A roofing or siding job involves several days of hard work, even with helpers.

If you fear being on a roof or high on a ladder, don't force yourself to do it. Discomfort with heights is a normal feeling. If you're determined to install your own roofing or siding, get accustomed to heights gradually, working your way up the ladder over a couple of days. If you still feel uneasy, hire a contractor to do the job.

Keep your cool while doing the job. When the work becomes frustrating, take a break. Working angry causes mistakes and accidents.

THE WORKER – PHYSICALLY

Prepare yourself for the physically demanding parts of this job. Shingling, particularly, and siding are hard work, requiring a lot of bending and lifting. Shingle bundles weigh about 80 pounds each. Even if you don't have to carry them up a ladder, you'll have to move them around on the roof.

Don't skimp on safety equipment. Doing the project yourself will probably save thousands of dollars. Buy good equipment and safe tools with part of your savings.

Wearing the right shoe is important. Rubber-soled leather work shoes or boots are best for working on roofs and ladders. They provide excellent wet and dry traction, the stiff sole lets you stand on a ladder rung without hurting the arch of your foot, and the leather uppers protect your feet. Athletic shoes aren't as good a choice, but they're better than shoes with hard, slick soles.

You'll be on your knees for most shingling. Get yourself and your helpers good kneepads—the ones covered with hard plastic or leather that will stand up to rough shingles.

Wear long-sleeve shirts and long pants. They should be loose and nonbinding so you can move about easily. Light-colored clothes are best. Shingles and the roof deck will become hot even in cooler weather. Also, most siding will reflect heat onto you.

Wear a hard hat when you're on the ground and work is going on above you. Even a single loose shingle can scrape you up if it falls from the roof. Wear a broad-brimmed hat at other times while working in the sun or on the roof. Use an appropriate sunblock.

Always wear gloves when working with metal roofing and siding or composition shingles. They have sharp edges and composition shingles often have pieces of metal from manufacturing embedded in them.

Wear protective glasses or goggles when nailing, because bits of metal can fly off. Put on safety eyewear when using a power saw to cut any roofing or siding material.

Have water or sport drinks available in quantity. Take frequent drinks while working to keep your body hydrated.

POWER NAILING

Renting a pneumatic roofing nailer and air compressor can cut the time of your roofing job in half. A power nailer can help on siding jobs, too. And it's a good way to avoid some smashed thumbs. However, such tools are capable of driving a three-inch nail into southern yellow pine at the pull of the trigger. Horsing around with one is dangerous. Even used properly, a power nailer can pose hazards for the unwary.

HERE ARE SOME SAFETY RULES FOR PNEUMATIC NAILERS:

■ The tool is commonly called a nail gun; treat the nailer as you would any gun. Consider the nail gun to be loaded and ready to fire all the time. Never pull the trigger unless you've placed the tip where you want to drive a nail.

■ Always wear the best polycarbonate safety glasses you can find.

■ Don't fool around, pretending to fire the nailer at other people or into the air.

■ Respect the tool's safety devices and don't attempt to circumvent them.

■ Keep your hands away from the tip where the nail comes out. There is no reason to have your hand closer than 3 inches from the tip. If a nail strikes a hidden roof decking nail, the tool can bounce and fire again. In some cases, the point of a nail can curl up out of the roof with enough force to pierce your hand.

■ Don't get so comfortable with the ease with which these tools can sink a nail that you begin firing them carelessly. Instead, get in the habit of waiting one second (count one one-thousand) from the time you place the nailer to the time you pull the trigger. You'll still save an average of five seconds per nail (more than 30 minutes per square) over nailing with a hammer.

■ You don't have to drive every nail on the roof with the nailer. In close quarters or around people, pound in a regular nail; they'll all be hidden anyway.

■ Be careful when you disconnect a pneumatic hose. Air pressure in the hose can whip the end around.

■ If the nailer jams, take it off the roof and away from people. Unload it before you fix it.

■ Bring the air hose from the compressor to the peak of the roof and secure it there with duct tape. Run the hose along the peak to a point near your work area. Secure the hose there, too, then run a coiled plastic hose down to the tool. In a similar fashion, run cords for electric tools along the ridge and down to the tools rather than up from the edge of the roof.

RULES OF THE ROOF

Knowing and following these few simple rules will help you to complete the job safely:

■ Keep your balance at all times. Overreaching on a roof or ladder can be dangerous.

■ Never go up on the roof when it is raining, when the roof is wet, or if there is a lightning storm. Work only when the weather is dry, with no strong winds.

■ Keep the roof clear of debris. Loose shingles and scraps of underlayment can slide. Watch for loose shingles or tiles, moss, and wet leaves.

■ When removing an old roof, work from the ridge down, and sweep the roof clean periodically.

■ Dump debris from the roof directly into a container or truck, if possible. For easy cleanup, avoid throwing materials into gardens or shrubbery.

■ Secure the area where you dump debris so no one strays into the falling-object zone. Keep pets, children, and bystanders away from your work area.

■ Keep your distance from the power line to your house.

■ Stack materials at the ridge of the roof and disperse them to spread the load. If the roof is steep, nail roofing jacks near the ridge on both sides and lay planks to keep the bundles in place.

■ If your roof has a slope of 5 in 12—about 22 degrees —or less (see page 22 for calculating roof slope), working comfortably should not be a problem.

■ On roofs with a steeper slope, you'll need to take some extra precautions. Apply the first few courses of a steep roof from a ladder with a ladder jack that holds one or two scaffold planks.

■ Use roof jacks on steeply sloped roofs.

■ Don't strain or overexert yourself. Lift just what is comfortable for you. It's better to split the load than cause a back injury.

■ Set a steady pace that's comfortable, and take frequent breaks to prevent fatigue. Quit when you're tired.

■ Don't get tangled in or trip over power cords or pneumatic air hoses.

SAFETY, FIRST AND LAST
continued

LADDERS, SCAFFOLDING, AND ROOFING JACKS

Ladders or scaffolding are essential for any siding job. Roofing calls for ladders and, sometimes, roofing jacks. All require caution at all times to avoid an accident.

LADDER CHOICES: An extension ladder is a basic tool for all roofing and siding. It allows you to climb to working heights and to carry material from the ground to where they are needed. Extension ladders are made of wood, aluminum, or fiberglass.

If you're going to buy a ladder, fiberglass is the best choice. Fiberglass ladders are light and strong, they flex slightly instead of

Scaffolding or a pair of extension ladders with ladder jacks provide safe work platforms. Ladder jacks hang on ladder rungs to support a plank. Install outriggers at the top of ladders for stability.

Outriggers

Planking

Planking

Ladder jacks

cracking, and they don't conduct electricity. They're the most expensive ladders.

Aluminum ladders are light and the strongest of ladders. They don't flex—a comfort for people who feel uneasy on ladders. However, they conduct electricity—keep them away from power lines.

Wood ladders are heavy. They flex over a long span, such as the climb to the gable of a roof. Many people don't like bouncing on a long wood ladder. Wood can rot and crack, which weakens the ladder.

LADDER SAFETY: Here are some guidelines for safe use of ladders:

■ Before using a ladder, inspect it to make sure it's in good condition, with no cracks or bends, and no loose screws or rivets.

■ Make sure that ropes, pulleys, and locking devices on extension ladders work properly.

■ Raise a long ladder by bracing the bottom against a heavy piece of lumber (a 6-foot 4×4 works great), then walking it up over your head from the other end.

■ When you raise a metal ladder, make sure that it does not come near the power line to your house. For roofing, there is no reason to have a ladder near a power line. For siding, don't raise the ladder high enough that it would fall into your power line.

■ Once the ladder is leaning against the house, set the base away from the house by a distance equal to one-fourth of the ladder's working height. Most new ladders have a sticker on the side that shows the correct angle.

■ Set the ladder on firm, level ground. If one leg must be shimmed to keep it level, use a single block of the correct height. Don't rest a ladder leg on stacked material.

■ Rubber feet prevent ladders from slipping on smooth concrete, decks, or tile. If you're using a ladder without rubber

CODES AND PERMITS

Before putting another roof over the old one, check how many already exist. Building codes generally require that a house have no more than three roofs on it. Because the third layer of shingles usually looks lumpy and bulky and some new roof decks are flimsier, more cities are limiting roof-overs to one after the original.

If you have 1,800 square feet of roof to cover with composite shingles weighing 240 pounds per square, that's more than 2 tons for each layer of shingles.

Some cities take this weight limit very seriously and have been known to require homeowners to remove a brand new roof because it didn't meet local code. Check your city codes before you start.

feet, buy safety shoes for it.
■ Extend a ladder to its working height only after it has been positioned properly against the house.
■ Never extend a ladder to more than 85 percent of its rated height. A long overlap between sections will make the ladder more stable.
■ When possible, have someone steady a ladder while you climb.
■ Only one person at a time should climb or stand on a ladder.
■ Stay off a ladder during bad weather or high winds.
■ Invest in a ladder brace that stabilizes it at the top, like outriggers.
■ Don't lean out from a ladder.
■ Lay a ladder on a steep roof to give yourself footing. Secure the ladder over the ridge of the roof with a metal ladder bracket.

SCAFFOLDING: Scaffolding speeds up a siding job by providing a work platform that allows you to work without moving ladders. However, the Occupational Safety and Health Administration (OSHA) warns that scaffolding is a leading cause of construction accidents. Scaffolding must be properly constructed for safety.

Welded pipe scaffolding is the sturdiest. It features a steel framework with adjustable feet, aluminum no-slip planks, and a built-in ladder. One person can erect or dismantle it.

Rent scaffolding from a local rental center; it fits easily in a pickup truck or can be delivered. Renting this scaffolding for a week may be cheaper than trying to build your own. However, if your project takes a long time, rental fees can add up.

For one-story siding, you can set up a simple scaffold with a pair of sturdy sawhorses and some wood planks. Make sure any wood plank extends 6 inches beyond its support to allow for bending and sliding.

Standard scaffolding is 12 feet long. Homemade scaffolding should be shorter—about 8 feet long—to increase safety.

For planks on sawhorse scaffolding, buy full 2-inch by 9-inch scaffold planks of rough-sawn spruce. (Many lumberyards sell these.) The rough surface prevents slipping, and the greater thickness makes the platform sturdier than standard 2× lumber. Place two planks side by side to form an 18-inch-wide platform—it's easier to stand on a wider surface when handling tools and materials. Cleat the planks together on the underside with three 16-inch-long pieces of 1×4.

For an alternate plank, nail two 7-foot 2×4s

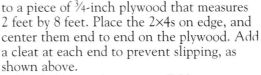

to a piece of ¾-inch plywood that measures 2 feet by 8 feet. Place the 2×4s on edge, and center them end to end on the plywood. Add a cleat at each end to prevent slipping, as shown above.

Stepladders make poor scaffold supports because they must be turned sideways to hold the plank and can easily tip or collapse.

To reach greater heights without scaffolding, rent ladder jacks that support a plank on two extension ladders (see the illustration on the opposite page).

ROOFING JACKS: Sometimes called roof brackets or toe-board jacks, roofing jacks are metal straps that hold a plank to provide a foothold on a steep roof (see the illustration below). Most of your weight stays on the roof, but the board prevents you from sliding down the slope. You also can walk back and forth on the roof, putting part of your weight on the board. Roofing jacks can be used on all types of roofing materials.

Notches on one end of the roofing jack are nailed to the roof; a bracket at the other end supports the step board. For safety, install a third roof jack in the middle of the span if you use a board longer than 10 feet.

Nail the roofing jacks securely to the roof with a regular 16-penny (16d) nail driven into a rafter. Always drive the nails where they will be covered by a subsequent course of shingles. When it's time to move the jack up, tap the bottom toward the roof ridge with a hammer to free it from the nail, then pound the exposed nail into the roof deck rather than pull it.

For siding a one-story house you can build an inexpensive scaffold with two sawhorses and a plank.

Roofing jacks hold a board on the roof to give an extra toehold. Use them on roofs with a slope of 6 in 12 or greater.

WHO WILL DO THE WORK?

You can repair your roof and install many kinds of siding yourself using the instructions in this book. However, before deciding to install a new roof, you need to consider additional factors.

ARE YOU UP TO IT?

How fast can you do the work? If you remove your old roof, you may have to work quickly to prevent rain from ruining your home. You can spread plastic sheeting to ward off sprinkles, but wind will rip it right off.

Roofing and siding are physically challenging. The work is hard, repetitious, sometimes hazardous, and usually hot and tiring. Materials, especially roofing, are heavy and have to be carried about. The steepness and height of your roof can be obstacles. If the roof is very steep or is two or more stories high and has dormers or a turret or two, you should hire a contractor.

Don't replace or install tar and gravel, slate, tile, or aluminum shingles yourself. Leave this work to the pros.

You'll work long hours, even with rented pneumatic tools. Calling in a professional to finish at a moment's notice will be at least as expensive as having the pro do the whole job.

Building inspectors and some suppliers are available only during regular business hours, and someone will have to be home during the week to work with them.

DO YOU HAVE THE TIME?

In estimating roofing time, allow two hours to put down the first square (100 square feet) of composition shingles. The second square will go a little faster, and by the second day, you might be putting down one square per hour. Double or triple these times for cedar shingles or shakes (see the chart on page 25). Other tasks will take time, such as taking delivery of materials, cleaning up, and removing the old roof, if necessary.

HOW TO HIRE A CONTRACTOR: If you decide to hire a contractor, find one you know or who has done a similar job well for a friend or neighbor. Otherwise, check the Yellow Pages or ask for names at local lumberyards and home centers. Except in smaller cities, general carpenters usually do not take on roofing jobs.

Contractors are licensed in most states, so you can check with the state contractors' licensing board about complaints. The contractor's contract must include the state license number. A contractor should be bonded, too, to assure that all work is completed satisfactorily. Ask for and check references for similar jobs.

Get the names of several professionals and ask them to bid on your job. Your bid request should spell out what work is to be done, who pays for the building permit, what materials are included, and whether disposal is required. Depending on local demand, you may be able

PROJECTS FOR THE DO-IT-YOURSELFER

TYPES OF ROOFS:
- Roofs on homes two stories or less
- Roofs with a slope of 8 in 12 or less (use roof jacks on slopes over 6 in 12)
- Gable roofs
- Dutch hip roofs
- Hip roofs
- Gambrel (barn) roofs (with scaffold for the steep portion)
- Mansard roofs (with scaffold)
- Shed roofs

INSTALLING ROOFING MADE OF:
- Composition shingles
- Cedar shakes or shingles
- Metal or panel roofs
- Rolled roofing (type with granules)

TYPES OF SIDING:
- Wood and wood-product horizontal siding
- Wood and wood-product panel siding
- Shingles
- Aluminum siding
- Vinyl siding
- Faux stone and stucco

DON'T GET SCAMMED

A confidence artist posing as a roofing or siding contractor can fleece an unwary homeowner out of thousands of dollars.

Beware of anyone who comes to your door soliciting work. Most reputable contractors do not sell their services door-to-door, though they sometimes distribute flyers. Always check out any contractor thoroughly before you hire work to be done.

SIGNS OF A REPUTABLE CONTRACTOR:
- Has company name on trucks, hats, coats, equipment
- Has a Yellow Pages listing or advertisement
- Licensed with the state
- Member of associations
- Has a local telephone number and it is answered with the company name
- Knows about building codes and permits

to negotiate a time-and-materials contract where you pay an hourly rate for labor and the actual cost of the materials. The advantage of such a contract is that you pay only the actual cost of the job. The disadvantage is you don't know the final cost until the end. Some roofing or siding contractors may be willing to let you help with the job, but most aren't interested in working with you if they must tutor you or correct your work.

SOLICITING BIDS: These guidelines will help you follow proper bidding etiquette.

■ Do not initiate a formal bid process if you already have a contractor in mind. Just negotiate a price with your chosen contractor.

■ Briefly describe the project in an initial telephone call to each contractor.

■ Get a recent reference for a job done by the same crew. Then check the reference and visit the home yourself. Also, call the Better Business Bureau to check on complaints.

■ After narrowing your choices to three or four contractors, set a date for receiving bids.

■ Specify what, if any, materials and labor you intend to provide.

■ Set an hourly rate for change orders. A change order is an agreement between the owner and contractor to modify the original plans once construction begins. Some contractors will bid the job low and try to make it up on change orders.

■ If a bidder asks for a clarification or you make a change after the initial bid, write it out. Send the information, labeled "Addendum," to each bidder.

■ Along with the price quote, get a copy of the contract form that the bidder uses. In some cases, the bid will serve as the contract.

ACCEPTING A BID: The low bid is not necessarily the best one to choose. Base the selection of a contractor on these factors:

■ Personal rapport
■ Experience
■ References and recommendations
■ Schedule
■ Cost

After bidding closes, it is unethical to negotiate simultaneously with two contractors or to ask other contractors to bid. After you accept a bid, notify all bidders of the winning price and thank them for bidding.

THE CONTRACT: The winning bidder should then provide a contract for the job that includes these items:

■ Agreement that the contractor will obtain building permits and perform all work according to applicable building codes

■ Start and completion dates, including allowances for weather and other delays

■ A clear outline of the contractor's duties

■ A statement that the contractor carries workers' compensation insurance, so you won't be liable if a worker is injured

■ An accounting of any materials you will supply and materials the contractor will supply, including brand or quality grades of the materials

■ A payment schedule. A quarter of the fee is often paid up front, another 50 percent is paid when the work actually begins, and the last quarter is paid after you and the building inspector are satisfied with the work—usually, two weeks after completion.

A complex, steep roof like this calls for a professional roofing job.

■ A provision requiring the contractor to provide lien releases from all subcontractors and suppliers before final payment is made. This ensures that these parties can't come back to you for payment.

■ A written guarantee that notes when the guarantee expires.

■ A procedure and rate for change orders.

■ The name of the person to contact on site with questions or problems during the project.

■ The method for resolving disputes.

BE YOUR OWN CONTRACTOR

If you have some business savvy, you may want to serve as your own contractor. This requires planning, seeing to the purchase and delivery of all materials, taking care of permits and inspections, providing some or all of the tools, and hiring skilled roofers—frequently known as specialists—to do the shingling. These roofers are usually excellent workers who don't want the responsibility of their own business and don't like working for other roofing contractors. Again, get references. You can save by hiring unskilled workers to strip an old roof.

What you don't pay is the profit the contractor expects to make on the job, which includes profit on all labor and materials. You can expect to save between 10 and 20 percent, but you'll earn it.

Good places to find roofing specialists include labor unions and your state's employment (unemployment) office. In a good economy, these specialists frequently begin their own small roofing business to take full advantage of the available work, so they might be hard to find.

Serving as your own contractor takes more time than hiring a professional contractor; you will probably have to take time off if you work outside the home. Ensure that the liability coverage of your homeowners insurance will be adequate. You also should check with the state about workers' compensation insurance. You may have to withhold and pay income and payroll taxes for the specialists and laborers you hire, too.

CHOOSING ROOFING MATERIALS

This chapter will help you select the right material for your roof and plan its installation. You'll find information about the variety of roof coverings available. You'll also find procedures for measuring your roof, determining its pitch, and figuring out how much roofing material you'll need to buy.

The important first step in roofing is choosing the right materials. You should consider how much money you're willing to spend and how long you want the roof to last. Factors such as how steep the roof is and the climate will affect your decision. Your home's color and style need to be considered, too, so you can maximize your home's value and the pride you take in it.

WHAT STYLE?

A new roof can change the way your house looks. A house of a particular style—Victorian or Spanish, for instance—calls for a roof that reflects that style. Roofs on homes older than 25 years probably aren't the originals, so simply replacing what is there isn't always the best option. You can often enhance an older home by replacing the existing roof with one more like the original. Or, you can choose roofing to give a plain-looking house a more distinctive look.

Dark-colored shingles with a texture that shows deep shadow lines add to the impact of this dramatic roof.

PRACTICAL CONSIDERATIONS

The slope of the roof limits your roofing choices. Some materials aren't suited to flat or low-pitched roofs. Cedar shingles and shakes, for instance, aren't recommended for roofs pitched lower than 3 in 12, and even at that pitch, a special installation method is required. Flat, low-pitched, and very steep roofs may require special installation techniques for most materials.

Climate affects your choice, too. Naturally rot-resistant cedar shingles and shakes left untreated will deteriorate in a particularly wet climate, such as the northwest United States. Panel roofs and three-tab shingles in high-wind areas, such as the Great Plains states, may blow off if not installed perfectly, and hail can damage composition roofing.

Once you know the practical limitations on your choice of roofing, take some time to study the remaining options. The photographs throughout this book can help you focus on possibilities. Lumberyards and home centers will give you product brochures and advice, and most manufacturers have Internet web sites.

A new roof will improve the look and value of your home. A radical contrast with the neighborhood norm or an unusual color combination, however, might decrease the value of your home and make your property an object of neighborhood scorn.

NEW CHOICES

You have many roofing choices today. Even composition shingles—the old standby—look better and last longer than ever before.

Thanks to well-placed shadows and color variations—and sometimes even an extra layer to enhance them—composition shingles can look like a shake roof. Drive down a street of established homes. You can practically see the difference in the age of roofs. Those that look like one solid color are probably older than color-variegated shingles with shadows.

You can choose how long a new roof will last; it just depends on how much you want to spend. Because labor is a major part of the cost of roofing—in money or sweat—spending twice as much on 40-year architectural-grade shingles could prove cheaper in the long run than buying standard 20-year shingles. If you plan to stay in your current house a long time, 40-year shingles may be the last roof covering you'll ever have to buy for it, too.

Steel roofing has become an attractive choice for residential roofing. Steel panels that look like Spanish tile, called Stile, are available nationwide. Other companies make panels that look like gray English slate or aged copper. Most makers of metal roofing now provide comprehensive lines of trim parts, making metal roofs look more complete. And modern metal roofing can last a lifetime. Professional installation is best.

Concrete shingles can look like slate, wood shakes, or shingles. They come in colors and weigh just a little more than composition shingles. Priced like shakes, they take longer to install. Professional installation is best for many styles, particularly on a complex roof.

Finally, several roofing products now on the market are manufactured from recycled materials such as reconstituted wood fibers, plastic, and aluminum.

HOW MUCH WILL IT COST?

New roofing is expensive, but necessary. In general, the better the material, the more it costs and the longer your roof will last. Slate, tile, and wood shake or shingle roofs are all beautiful, but are expensive. You can often halve the cost of a wood shake or shingle roof by applying it yourself. It takes some skill and hard work, but you can do it with a little knowledge, patience, and perseverance.

Composition shingles—even the premium-grade ones that look like shakes—are ideal for do-it-yourself installations.

The chart on page 25 will give you some idea of relative costs. Prices vary around the country and are subject to change, but this chart should give you an idea of how much a roof will cost if you know the size of the roof in squares (see page 23 for instructions on figuring this) and the cost of popular shingles at a home center or lumberyard (check your Sunday newspaper supplements).

ASK A REAL ESTATE AGENT

Need another opinion? Real estate professionals hear the likes and dislikes of their customers and develop a sense of what buyers want. They can tell you what kind of roofs attract favorable—or unfavorable—attention in your area. Call the agent who sold you your house or another who knows your neighborhood.

TYPES OF ROOFING MATERIALS

WOOD SHINGLING PATTERNS

Straight

Staggered

FANCY CUT WOOD SHINGLES

Scallop or fish scales

Angled or cut scallop

Roofing comes in a wide range of materials. Wood, metal, tile, and other materials offer different qualities. Here are some of the choices.

COMPOSITION SHINGLES

More than 70 percent of the houses in the United States are roofed with composition shingles, according to some estimates. For years, these shingles were made of plain asphalt and paper and called asphalt shingles. Today's composition shingles have a central core of cellulose fibers or fiberglass that is coated with modified asphalt on both sides and topped with protective mineral granules. These shingles have a Class A fire rating. They come in a wide array of colors, weights, textures, and styles.

Three-tab composition shingles are the easiest for the do-it-yourselfer to apply. Usually they are 12 inches wide and 36 inches long. They are packaged three or four bundles to a square (100 square feet of coverage). The shingles also come in similar metric dimensions, but don't try to mix metric and inch shingles on a roof. (The instructions in this book use inches and feet.)

Composition shingles also come in two-tab, one-tab, or interlocking styles, but these variations are usually for special applications like barns and other large buildings.

Asphalt shingles used to be graded primarily by their weight per square—heavier shingles lasted longer. Today's composition shingles are rated by warranty term. Typical inexpensive, one-color shingles are warranted for 20 years.

Modern composition shingles have strips of roofing cement that seal each shingle to the one above it. The sun heats the strip and

bonds the two shingles together, even in winter. Once cemented together, shingles are unlikely to blow off. In one recorded case, strong straight-line winds blew down a building, but the roofing remained bonded together—not a shingle was lost.

WOOD SHINGLES AND SHAKES

Wood shingles are smaller and lighter than shakes and are usually sawn on both sides, which gives them a smooth surface. Shakes are split rather than sawn, which gives them a rougher appearance. Both shingles and shakes are made from western red cedar.

Shakes and shingles are graded #1 (the best), #2, and #3. Use only #1 shingles for the roof of a house. Cut from heartwood, they are highly resistant to rot and are free of knots. For sheds and other secondary buildings or for siding, #2 shingles are adequate.

Shingles and shakes from old-growth wood have been known to last 50 years untreated. Today's shingles, from newer, sustainable forests, will last about half as long if untreated. Modern wood preservatives will greatly extend the life of cedar roofing.

Shingles and shakes come in 16- and 18-inch lengths. The most common are 18 inches long. They are sold in bundles, with four to seven bundles per square.

Untreated shingles and shakes are usually applied over spaced 1×4s or 1×6s rather than over a solid-sheathed roof to allow air to circulate. Shakes always have underlayment (see page 21) over the roof deck beneath them. Their irregular surface allows air to circulate. Underlayment is used under untreated shingles only in regions where ice may build up, and then only along the edges of the roof. You can lay wood shingles over a solid roof deck or open sheathing with full underlayment if you give the shingles periodic waterproofing treatments.

CLAY AND CONCRETE TILES

A Spanish clay tile roof looks great and will last as long as the house. But the tiles weigh more than a thousand pounds per square—even more when wet—and most roofs need reinforcement to hold the weight.

Concrete tiles are challenging clay tiles in popularity now. Concrete tiles are cheaper, easier to install, and lighter (750 to 900 pounds per square). They come in a variety of colors and shapes—barrel-shaped like mission tiles, flat, ribbed, or S-curved. Some special varieties of concrete tile are light enough to go on a standard roof. Each concrete tile is molded with a ridge on the back that hooks over spaced sheathing or cleats.

Clay and concrete tiles are much more expensive and difficult to apply than composition shingles. If you are considering a tile roof, most distributors will send a representative to evaluate the roof and recommend additional framing that may be needed. Installation is not a job for the average homeowner. The danger of damage to the home because of weight or improper installation greatly outweighs any possible savings in labor.

SLATE

Like tile, slate roofs are expensive and heavy, but will last a lifetime. Slate for roofs comes from a natural laminated rock that has been split into shingles. Slate makes a beautiful roof and is fireproof. Because of its weight and the complexity of installation, it should be professionally installed.

METAL ROOFS

Aluminum and steel roofing panels are inexpensive, long lasting, and relatively easy to install. Metal roofs are noisy in a rainstorm and worse in a hailstorm. Old-fashioned corrugated steel sheets are rarely used for residential roofs; more stylish panels are painted and ribbed. Aluminum panels are strong, will not rust, and are easy to transport and cut. Cheap, thin aluminum panels will dent in a hailstorm.

Metal sheets joined by a standing seam form the most durable metal roof. A homeowner can install this type on a simple roof under ideal conditions. For instance, many companies sell panels cut to length. For a standard gable roof, it's simple to cut

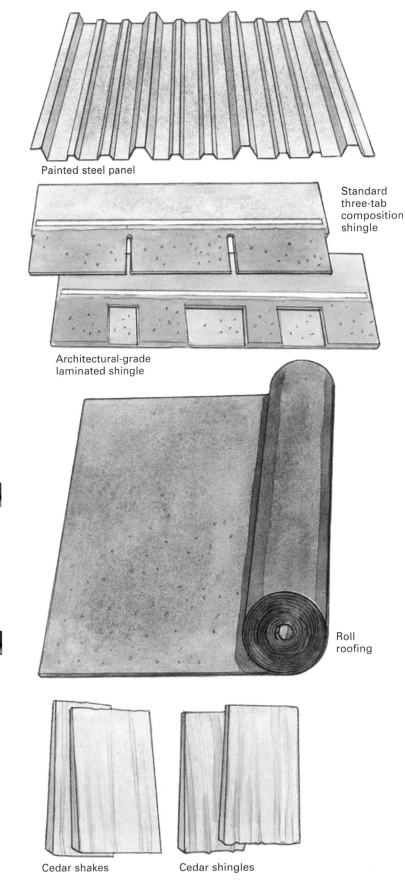

Painted steel panel

Standard three-tab composition shingle

Architectural-grade laminated shingle

Roll roofing

Cedar shakes

Cedar shingles

TYPES OF ROOFING MATERIALS
continued

these panels to fit around vents and the chimney and attach them to the roof. Many of the styled steel roofs that look like tile or slate are custom cut. A professional should install them on any complicated roof that has numerous valleys and dormers.

Be careful when handling steel panels; the edges are sharp. Panels that fall off of a roof or blow around in the wind pose a hazard.

Metal panels conduct heat readily, so they require insulation underneath. Metal panels expand and contract with temperature changes, too.

Panels are usually attached by screws or nails with rubber washers. Aluminum shingles are increasingly popular because of their fire-resistant qualities and long life. They are expensive, but will last the life of the house. Aluminum shingles are difficult to apply correctly, so you should have them installed by a professional.

Copper roofs are beautiful and last a long time. They slowly turn from the color of a freshly minted penny to an antique green. Every shade is beautiful in its own right. Copper comes in panels or shingles and is among the most expensive and difficult of roof materials to install. If you can afford a copper roof, you can afford to have it installed professionally.

CONCRETE-FIBER SHINGLES

Like slate and clay tiles, concrete-fiber shingles can last a lifetime. They're lighter than slate or tile because they're thinner—

lightweight fibers are used as fillers and strengtheners in the concrete. They're reasonably priced. However, they're hard and brittle so it takes more time to install them. If you have a smaller house and want a permanent roof, this may be a good choice. But it could take you a whole day to install one square. If you have a 2,500-square-foot home with an attached three-car garage, it would be a lengthy project.

MINERAL ROLL ROOFING

This is essentially the same material as composition shingles, but in a roll 36 inches wide and 36 feet long—about one square. It's usually installed as roofing only on secondary buildings. It can be used as a flashing material or under metal flashing, too.

Roll roofing doesn't last as long as shingles because it is installed with a small overlap, giving the roof just one layer of protection. Shingles are overlapped in such a way that they provide two or three layers over the roof. Installed with an 18-inch overlap, roll roofing can provide the same durability as shingles, and will cost just as much.

Selvage-edge rolls are also called split-sheet roofing because they are smooth on the upper half and mineral covered on the lower half. When the roofing is applied, the mineral-covered surface overlaps all the smooth surface of the strip below. This overlap—along with some adhesive—provides excellent protection on very low-slope roofs. Two rolls of this roofing cover one square.

TAR AND GRAVEL

This roof, often called a hot-mopped or built-up roof, is primarily useful for low-pitched roofs. It consists of alternating layers of roofing felt and hot tar with a protective coat of gravel.

When a tar and gravel roof becomes worn— after about 15 years—another one can be put directly over it.

Replacing a built-up roof is a job for professionals. It requires specialized equipment and is hot, heavy, miserable work.

Cold-mopped roofing is an inexpensive—but less-effective—method of applying a built-up roof. The tar goes on as a liquid so it doesn't have to be heated. Cold-mopped roofing is usually used for repair work.

FIRE RESISTANCE OF ROOFING MATERIALS

Roofing materials are rated as class A, B, or C for fire resistance by Underwriter's Laboratories (UL), an independent testing service. Class A is the highest rating. Manufacturers display the UL rating prominently on each bundle of shingles.

COMPOSITION SHINGLES: Look for a Class A rating on composition shingles. Don't install composition shingles that don't carry a UL rating.

WOOD SHINGLES AND SHAKES: Unless treated with a retardant, shakes and wood shingles are flammable. The UL-approved, fire-retardant, pressure-treated shakes and wood shingles are more expensive but are safer in fire-risk areas. They may be required by local building codes. However, some cities ban wood shingle roofs on the basis that even treated wood is not sufficiently fire resistant.

Slate, tile, concrete-fiber shingles, and metal panels: These materials are not just fire resistant; they're actually fireproof. However, metal has a lower fire rating because it conducts heat so readily.

ROLL ROOFING: Both types of this material are fire resistant. Prolonged exposure to fire, however, would eventually cause them to burn.

UNDERLAYMENT

Underlayment is the asphalt-impregnated felt laid under most roofing materials as a secondary water barrier. Felt is classified by weight per square, usually 15- or 30-pound. A roll usually covers two or four squares.

ADDITIONAL SUPPLIES

Measure the diameter of all vent pipes, and buy the metal and neoprene rubber flashing units that slip over them.

If flashing is needed around a chimney or skylight, measure along the roofline to determine how much is needed.

You will need roofing cement in caulking-gun tubes. It also comes in larger quantities, but the tube is easiest to use. For every 10 squares of roof surface, get four tubes of roofing cement. If you have a steep roof, you will need one tube for every square, plus the additional four tubes mentioned above. Keep the tubes dry. If you don't use it all, return them.

Buy two tubes of butyl rubber or silicone caulk for every 10 squares to use around flashings or valleys.

For nails, allow 2 pounds per square for composite shingles, concrete shingles, and cedar shingles or shakes. If you plan to use pneumatic nailers or staplers, you'll have to buy the special nails or staples in a box of 5,000 nails or 10,000 staples. Nails are slightly better in high-wind areas, and staples are much cheaper. At four nails or staples per composition shingle and 100 shingles to a typical square, 10,000 staples are enough for 25 squares and 5,000 nails will secure a little more than 12 squares. If you're going to rent air tools, contact your local rental center to find out what brand they have. Different brands use different nails.

Be prepared for rain. Make sure that you have some rolls of 6-mil plastic sheeting on hand to spread over the roof, and 1×4 boards or a bundle of plaster lath to tack it down so the wind won't rip it away.

For composition shingles, first lay a starter roll. This mineral-coated asphalt roofing material comes in a roll about 8 inches wide. The strip nails down at the edge of the eaves and the shingles are laid over it. It provides needed roof protection under the first row of shingles. It's cheaper than using shingles for the first course and is better than the old roofer's trick of installing a first course of shingles upside down.

With wood shingles and shakes, instead of using a starter roll, double the first course of shingles. Roll roofing and metal and vinyl panels don't need a starter.

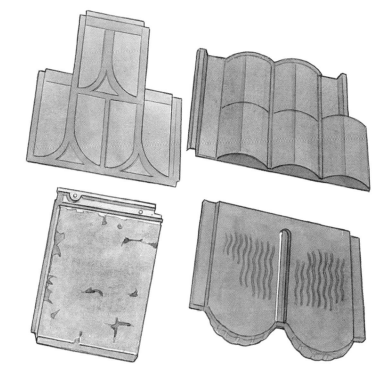

Long-life shingles, made from steel, aluminum, concrete, recycled materials, and composites, come in many styles.

If you're stripping your roof, replace or cover the underlayment. In areas where snow builds up on the roof, install a special ice barrier underlayment at the eaves. On a house with a 4-pitch roof, install one course. A low-pitched roof requires 2½ courses of the barrier.

It's also a good idea to replace the roof venting and flashing if you're stripping your roof. Roof vents come in various styles. Consider them worn out if the insect screens are torn or missing. Flashing is not expensive and using old flashing that's been removed from your old roof isn't worth the grief of dealing with kinked and bent metal.

For metal roofing, you will need special self-drilling screws with rubber washers, nails with rubber washers under the heads, or special fasteners sold by the company that makes the roofing. Most styled-steel roofs also have matching flashing and trim pieces to fit in the valleys and along the ridge and eaves.

CORRECT NAIL OR STAPLE LENGTH

Roof nails or staples turn cold and moisture condenses on them. If the fasteners go completely through the roof deck, this moisture drops onto the insulation. Although this water probably won't find its way into the home, it degrades the insulation and can lead to rot, mold, and mildew.

The ideal nail or staple is just long enough to go through all the layers of shingles on a roof and stop just short of going through the roof deck. For instance, if you're putting regular single-ply shingles on a new ½-inch plywood roof deck, you'll want nothing longer than ¾-inch nails. If you're reroofing with laminated shingles on an older home that has ¾-inch boards, you might use nails or staples 1¼ inches long.

ESTIMATING AND ORDERING MATERIALS

Before you can order materials for your roofing job, you need to measure your roof and figure the area. Here's how to do that, along with some hints on purchasing your roofing.

SLOPE

Slope, or pitch, is the change in roof height (the rise) for a horizontal distance (the run). It is usually expressed as 4 in 12, for instance, where 4 inches is the rise and 12 inches is the run. The slope of your roof may influence your choice of roofing material. A lower-pitched roof requires more precautions to avoid leaks because the flatter a roof is, the slower it sheds water. Metal panels and composite shingles can be put on slopes as low as 2 in 12 with a special low-pitch

There are two ways of determining pitch. Lay a board on the roof to get an accurate surface angle. Mark a level 12 inches from the end. Place the level on the board and lift the lower end until it's level. Then measure the distance from the mark on the level to the board with a ruler. The other way is to determine the angle of the roof with a degree indicator. Once you determine the angle, you can find the slope on the chart at right.

installation (see page 45). Slopes of 1 in 12 to 2 in 12 are best covered with selvage-edge roll roofing. Professionally installed soldered metal, built-up roofing, or an elastomer (rubber) membrane are the only choices for a flat roof.

Slopes normally range from 1 in 12 (nearly flat) to 12 in 12 (a 45-degree angle—typical of an A-frame) to even 16 in 12 on some mansard roofs. You don't need to determine the slope precisely. You just need to know whether it is unusually low—less than 4 in 12, requiring special installation—or steeper than 8 in 12, which can be difficult to work on. A typical modern suburban home (built in the past 25 years) probably has a 4 in 12 or a 6 in 12 roof pitch.

DETERMINING THE SLOPE: There are two easy ways to determine roof slope. You'll have to climb up on the roof or work from a ladder for either method.

■ The easiest way is to measure the slope directly, using a straight 3-foot board, a carpenter's level, and a ruler. To do this, lay the board flat on the roof, running straight up and down the slope. Mark a point on the level 12 inches from one end, then place the end of the level from where you measured near the top of the board. Raise the other end, as shown in the illustration at left, until level. Hold the ruler perpendicular to the level at the 12-inch mark, and measure from the board to the bottom of the level. If the distance is 6 inches, for example, it means that the roof rises 6 inches in 12 inches of horizontal run—a 6 in 12 pitch. If it's 4 inches, then it's a 4 in 12 pitch.

ANGLE VS. PITCH

Angle		Pitch
60.25°	=	21 in 12
59.0°	=	20 in 12
56.25°	=	18 in 12
53.0°	=	16 in 12
49.5°	=	14 in 12
45.0°	=	12 in 12
39.75°	=	10 in 12
33.75°	=	8 in 12
30.25°	=	7 in 12
26.5°	=	6 in 12
22.5°	=	5 in 12
18.5°	=	4 in 12
14.0°	=	3 in 12
9.5°	=	2 in 12
4.75°	=	1 in 12

■ Another method is to measure the angle of the roof and translate that angle into a pitch, using the chart (opposite page).

You can measure the angle easily with a bubble protractor—a round dial with a level vial in the center. Some dealers call them dial levels, degree indicators, or angle finders. To gauge the roof angle with one, put a 3-foot straight board on the roof, set the tool on the board, as shown at the bottom of the opposite page, and turn the inner dial until the bubble shows level. Read the angle at the pointer.

You also could use the carpenter's triangular rafter square, usually called by one of its brand names (the Speed Square), and a small level. The rafter square has one lipped edge, a pivot point at one corner, and a degree scale on the opposite edge. A high-quality one costs about $10 and ranks as one of the handiest of carpenter's layout tools. You can measure the roof angle at the rake end with one. Lay the top of the lipped edge of the rafter square on the roof (or a 3-foot board laid on the roof), with the square corner toward the top of the slope, as shown in the illustration on the following page. Set a level on top of the lipped edge, and pivot the square up to level. Read the angle where the roof edge crosses the scale.

CALCULATING ROOF AREA: The easiest way to calculate roof area is to get up on the roof and measure it. Round your measurements to the next foot— this makes figuring easier and is precise enough for making a materials estimate.

Treat a simple gable roof as a pair of rectangles. To find the area of a rectangle, multiply the length times the width. Measure along the ridge or eaves to find the length and from the ridge to the eaves to find the width. Multiply them together to get the area of one side of the roof in square feet, then double it for the whole roof.

Divide complicated roofs into rectangles and triangles for easy figuring. To find the area of a triangle, multiply height times base width, then divide by 2 ([height × base] / 2 = area).

If your roof is difficult to clamber onto, make your roof estimate from the ground. Measure the roof as if its edges were projected on the ground, then correct for the amount of slope in the roof by using the area/rake conversion chart on this page.

Using the house shown at right as an example, first measure the outline of the house from eave to eave. Include roof overhangs—

don't just measure from wall to wall. Draw the roof outline on paper, and add the ridge, dormers, porch, and chimney.

You now have on paper an outline of your house as if it had a flat roof. Because the roof slopes, it actually covers more area than shown on the flat drawing.

■ Now, figure out the area of the roof from the drawing. Divide the roof into rectangles and triangles. Deduct areas for the chimney and skylights. The dormer can be calculated

EAVES, RIDGES, AND RAKES CONVERSION

Slope*	Rake/Area Factor
4	1.054
5	1.083
6	1.118
7	1.157
8	1.202
9	1.250
10	1.302
11	1.356
12	1.414

* inches per foot

If it's difficult to get on the roof, measure the lengths of walls and overhangs to find the size of the roof as if it were flat. Then, knowing the pitch, use the chart at left to estimate the roof area accurately enough to order materials.

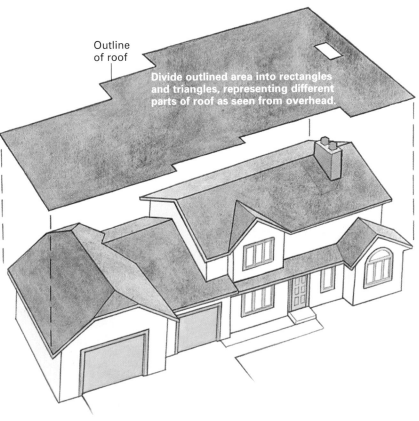

Outline of roof

Divide outlined area into rectangles and triangles, representing different parts of roof as seen from overhead.

ESTIMATING AND ORDERING MATERIALS
continued

An inexpensive triangular roofing square and a short level provide a simple way to determine the roof slope. Tilt the roofing square until the top is level. Read the degree mark from the scale and see the chart on page 22 to determine the slope. You can place a board on the roof to create a flat base.

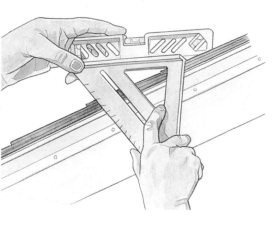

separately; but if you just have one or two, include these as part of the gross roof area and you will be close enough.

In this example there are 1,294 square feet in the main roof and 640 in the L-roof.

■ Determine the slope of your roof sections. (See page 22.) Be aware that different parts of the roof can have different slopes.

■ Find the conversion factor on the area/rake conversion chart.

■ Then multiply the total number of square feet on your drawing by the conversion factor.

For the main 9-pitch roof of 1,294 square feet, multiply it by the rake factor of 1.250. That equals 1,617 square feet. For the L-roof with a 6 in 12 slope, multiply the 640 square feet by 1.118 to arrive at 715 square feet. Add them for the total, which is 2,333 square feet.

HIP AND VALLEY CONVERSION

Hip/Valley Slope	Factor
4	1.452
5	1.474
6	1.500
7	1.524
8	1.564
9	1.600
10	1.642
11	1.684
12	1.732

ROOFING CEMENT IS NOT CAULK

Professional roofers frequently apply black roofing cement as a caulk around flashing and valleys. It holds up alright, but it wasn't designed to be a caulk. It's made to glue shingles together and glue down flashings to increase the overall strength of the roof.

Where you need caulking, black butyl rubber caulk, silicone caulk, or neoprene roofing cement—a product designed for double-duty—will last longest. Although they're more expensive, they expand and contract well, which is what you need to better protect your house.

■ Whether you measure directly or figure from the conversion charts, add 10 percent for waste. That makes a total of 2,566 square feet for our diagram.

■ Divide that by 100 to find the number of squares (25.7 in the example). Round that up (26 in the example). This is the number you'll use to figure costs and to order underlayment and most shingles and shakes.

EAVES, RIDGES, AND RAKES: Measure for other materials, such as drip edge and ridge shingles. Eaves—the bottom edge of a roof—and the ridge—the top edge of the roof—can be measured directly without using a conversion chart. For most gable roofs, the eaves will be the same length as the ridge.

Measure the rakes, or the downward sloping sides of the roof, directly, or calculate the length from your drawing. To do that, find the horizontal distance and multiply it by the conversion factor in the chart for the slope of your roof. Add the length of the rakes to the eave measurements to find the total drip edge needed. The length of the ridge will tell you the quantity of ridge shingles and ridge vents to get.

HIPS AND VALLEYS: These involve sloped distances, so another chart (left) comes into play. Find the horizontal distances of hips and valleys on your drawing by noting how far they extend into the roof (for example, one half or one third). Then, using the overall width of the roof, estimate the number of feet. Multiply that distance by the conversion factor shown for your roof slope on the chart at left.

With these figures, your roofing supplier can provide the proper lengths of valley flashing and quantities of hip shingles.

METAL OR PANEL ROOFS: If you plan to install a metal or panel roof, don't rely on estimation. Measure the roof directly. That's because the best way to order this kind of roofing is custom cut to length. The panels are easier to install and look better when cut accurately, squarely, and uniformly.

You need exact dimensions when ordering precut panel roofing. If the panels are too long, you'll have a lot of metal cutting to do, unless the panels overlap and you can take up the extra at the joint. And, buying all of the panels cut an inch or so too short would be even worse. If your roofing dealer offers a measuring service, take advantage of it even for a fee. The dealer has experience in measuring roofs and can take the needed measurements accurately. In case of an error, it will cost the dealer, not you. If you have a roof with valleys or other complicated features, hire a professional to install the panels.

HOW TO BUY ROOFING

Once you have a list of your estimated material needs in hand, contact several lumberyards or home centers and get prices.

THINGS YOU SHOULD CONSIDER:

■ Price the materials individually. Some places offer shingles at a low price, then charge high prices for the rest of the supplies.

■ Include delivery charges in the total price.

■ Arrange for rooftop delivery so you don't have to carry the roofing up a ladder. If no companies in your area offer rooftop delivery, plan to rent a hoist or conveyor to get your supplies onto the roof.

■ Set a precise delivery date—at least narrow it down to morning or afternoon of a certain day. Don't buy from roofing dealers who give vague delivery schedules.

■ If you're stripping a roof, buy from a store with the most flexible delivery service. That way, you can call for same-day or next-day delivery when you're ready.

■ Get materials delivered as close to your work time as possible. Avoid storing anything because you'll have to keep it dry.

ESTIMATED TIME VS. COST

Roofing Material	Cost Factor*	Est. D-I-Y time in hours per square**
20-year composition shingles	1.0	2.2 hours
20-year roll roofing w/granules	0.8	2.4 hours
25-year composition shingles	1.35	2.4 hours
Painted ribbed-steel roofing	3.0	4.8 hours
Styled steel roofing	6.0	4.8 hours
Split cedar shakes#	7.25	4.8 hours
Sawn cedar shingles#	8.8	6 hours
Concrete shingles	3.4	9 hours

Doesn't include underlayment, fasteners, flashing, or edge, which changes from roof to roof.

**This is estimated by taking the professional rate and multiplying by 1.5 and includes time in a typical day not spent on the task. Increase the time by an additional 50 percent for steep roofs.*

 # Includes the cost of fire retardant.

For example, for a small 12×16' garage (three squares) and using a 20-year composition shingle cost of $30 per square, the cost would be $90, plus roofing felt and nails, and would take about 6.6 hours.

ROOFER'S HATCHET

A regular claw hammer works fine for most roofing jobs. But a roofer's hatchet is a must with cedar shakes and shingles. That's because you don't cut shakes and shingles; you split them.

The roofer's hatchet offers two other handy tools:

■ **AN EXPOSURE GAUGE:** A knob fits into a hole in the blade to gauge the shingle exposure.

■ **A COMPOSITE SHINGLE CUTTER:** The cutting blade is replaceable or can be sharpened.

While these tools are handy, many roofers get by with a simple wooden roofer's jig (page 40) as an exposure guide and notched utility knife blades for cutting composite shingles. The blades are cheap and disposable.

COORDINATING COLORS

The color of the roof should complement the trim and siding. This chart offers some suggestions for appropriate color combinations.

With today's multicolored shingles, it's also possible to choose a shingle with many colors. For instance, several companies offer a multicolored slate look with blacks, grays, reds, and browns. Several companies also offer brownish shingles with some tabs in black and tan.

Otherwise, there are four basic colors in solid-colored roofs. They are white, black, weathered cedar gray, and new cedar tan.

House Color	Roof Color
White	White, black, brown, green, gray, red, beige
Ivory	Black
Beige	Brown, green
Taupe	White, black, tan
Brown	Brown, green, tan
Yellow	White, black, gray, brown, green
Deep gold	Black
Coral pink	White, black, gray
Dull red	Gray, red
Light blue	Red
Gray-blue	White, blue
Medium blue	Black, brown, dark blue
Deep blue	Gray
Light green	White, gray, red, brown, dark green, tan
Olive green	White, black
Dark green	Gray, beige
Gray	White, black, dark gray, red, green
Charcoal	White

INSTALLING YOUR NEW ROOF

Roofing over an existing roof eliminates the need for underlayment and saves the time and effort of tearing off the old roof. However, if the old one is too irregular for a smooth finish, tear it off. Otherwise, the new one won't look right and won't protect as well.

Roofs are heavy; local codes may permit as many as three layers or may limit you to two. Check before you decide to simply layer over the existing roof.

ROOFING OVER AN OLD ROOF

Roofing over an existing roof eliminates the need for underlayment and saves you the time and trouble of tearing off

the old roof. However, if the old one is too irregular for a smooth finish, tear it off. It won't look right and it won't protect as well.

Remember, roofs are heavy. Some local codes permit as many as three layers, others may limit you to two. (See the Guidelines for Covering Old Roofing chart on page 28.)

COVERING COMPOSITION SHINGLES WITH MORE SHINGLES: Any irregularities in the existing roof must be repaired in order to produce a smooth roof. Warped or bent shingles should be split and nailed flat. Missing shingles must be replaced so there won't be a sag in that spot.

When covering an existing roof of composition shingles, it's best to match the shingling pattern already used on the old roof.

The first step in roofing over an existing asphalt roof is to apply a starter strip along the eaves. Measure the shingle exposure on the existing roof (usually 5 or 6 inches). If the existing shingle does not extend far enough out to spill water into the gutter, add enough to your measurement so the new ones will.

In many cases, you can install your own roof and save the cost of labor.

Using whole new shingles, cut the tabs off. Then measure up from the newly trimmed edge to match the exposure in the old roof, plus any small addition to spill water into the gutter. Cut them again at this point. They should now fill the exposure and be level with the old second course. Nail them in place with the adhesive strip adjacent to the eaves. Cut enough starter shingles to go along all the eaves. Discard the tab ends.

On a 5-inch exposure roof, remove 2 inches from the top of shingles used for the next course and butt them up against the bottom of the old third course. This 10-inch shingle covers the starter course and the second course on the old roof. Cut enough of these 10-inch-wide shingles to run the length of the eaves.

For a 6-inch exposure, apply a full shingle to cover the 6-inch-wide starter strip and the second course.

Now cut 5 or 6 inches—depending on the old roof's shingling pattern—off the rake side of the next shingle and butt it up against the bottom of the fourth course of old shingles. This second course will leave a 3-inch exposure on the first course. This will probably not be noticeable. If you have a steep roof, where this course can easily be seen, trim 1 inch from the top of the second and third courses. This will give the first and second courses a 4-inch exposure, which will be less noticeable. On either of these with a shorter exposure, put a dab of cement under each shingle that sits on top of it. The second method requires more cutting and more cementing.

For all remaining courses, cut and apply just as you would for a new roof. The exposure follows automatically, because all new shingles butt up against existing courses. You'll probably use longer nails—1-inch nails with a ½-inch plywood deck or 1¼-inch nails with full ¾-inch decking.

COVERING TAR AND GRAVEL WITH COMPOSITION SHINGLES:
You should remove a built-up roof rather than shingling over it. If you must shingle over one, however, prepare the roof by removing the gravel and nailing down any bubbles. Another option is to lay fanfold insulation—typically applied under siding—over the gravel. This will smooth the surface so the

COVERING COMPOSITION SHINGLES WITH WOOD SHINGLES

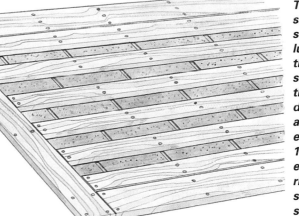

To reduce shingle rot, nail strips of 1×4 lumber on top of the composition shingles. Space them the same distance apart as the shingle exposure. Nail 1×6s along the eaves, rakes, and ridges. Nail the shingles to the strips.

COVERING WOOD SHINGLES WITH COMPOSITION SHINGLES

To cover wood shingles without removing them, nail on some horsefeathers—long, tapered boards—to level out the butts of the shingles. Remove enough shingles to nail down flat 1×6s along the eaves, rakes, and ridges.

new roof won't look lumpy. Reroofing will also require a change in drip edge, from one designed to keep gravel in place to one made for shedding water. Once prepared, shingle the roof as you would a stripped roof.

COVERING WOOD SHINGLES WITH WOOD SHINGLES OR SHAKES:
It's best to install shakes over old wood shingles because there is less likelihood of leaks and rot. If you use wood shingles, make sure they've been treated with a preservative.

If the old wood shingles on a roof are in good condition, you can lay new wood shingles over them. Some preliminary steps are still necessary. First, nail down any curled or warped shingles to provide an even surface. If one won't stay down, split it, pull out the pieces, and slip in a new shingle.

Remove shingles along the eaves, rakes, and ridges, and replace them with 1×6 boards. To do this, measure 5½ inches back from the edges of the rakes and eaves, then snap a chalk line as a cutting guide.

ROOFING OVER AN OLD ROOF
continued

Set the blade on a circular saw just slightly beyond the shingle depth, and cut. Use an old saw blade or one specially made for remodeling, because you will hit some nails. Follow the same procedure on both sides of the ridge.

Sweep the roof, then nail down the 1×6 boards along the eaves and rakes. At the ridge, use a length of cedar bevel siding, with the thin edge on the down side. Apply new flashing in the valleys.

With the surface prepared, follow standard shingling procedures for the new roof.

WOOD SHINGLES OVER OTHER ROOFS:
Applying wood shingles over composition shingles, roll roofing, and tar and gravel roofs is quite similar to new shingling. Shingles must be laid over spaced sheathing nailed directly to the existing roof.

For an asphalt roof, remove the shingles along the ridge and hips. Removal isn't needed with roll roofing or tar and gravel.

Trim the ends and edges of existing composition shingles where they overhang the rakes and eaves. You can cut them with tin snips or a utility knife.

Next, nail 1×6 boards along the rakes, from ridge to eaves. This provides a finished edge when the shingles are in place. Nail 1×6s along the eaves and on both sides of the ridge, with the edges of the boards meeting at the ridge. Finally, nail 1×4 boards down each side of the valleys to provide support for the new valley flashing that must be installed. Place spaced 1×4s over the roof, spaced the same as your shingle exposure. (See page 47 for detailed instructions.)

Before shingling, lay the valley flashing in place, as described on pages 30 and 31. Now shingle the roof in a standard fashion, as described earlier.

PANEL ROOFS OVER OTHER ROOFS:
Panel roofs can go on top of a variety of roofs, except other panel roofs. Remove the existing panels before installing new ones.

GUIDELINES FOR COVERING OLD ROOFING

OLD COMPOSITION SHINGLES
You can install the following new roofs on an old composition shingle roof that is worn but relatively flat (nail down warped shingles and replace missing ones):
- Composition shingles
- Shakes
- Metal roofing

OLD TAR AND GRAVEL
This roof probably has a pitch of 4 in 12 or less, which limits your choices. Check the edge to see how many layers of gravel exist, with each one representing a new roof. If you find two or less, you can probably apply another roof. However, if the gravel is left in place, most roofing products won't lie flat.

IF YOU REMOVE MOST OF THE GRAVEL, YOU CAN INSTALL:
- Composition shingles (a pitch of 2 in 12 or greater)
- Shakes (a pitch of 3 in 12 or greater)
- Metal roofing
- Roll roofing

WOOD SHINGLES
If the roof is in good condition but uneven, you can improve it by nailing beveled strips of wood, commonly called horsefeathers or feathering strips.

YOU COULD THEN COVER THE ROOF WITH:
- Composition shingles
- Shakes

- Metal panels

Before you nail on a new cedar shingle roof over the old, it's best to nail on additional 1×4s to provide good air circulation. That's why shakes are popular as a second layer for shingle roofs.

SHAKES
A shake roof is too irregular to cover with anything new. You'll have to tear it off.

ROLL ROOFING
Assuming an adequate slope and a relatively even surface, you can install:
- Roll roofing
- Composition shingles
- Shakes
- Metal roofing

Wood shingles usually require spaced 1×4 sheathing boards, and new roll roofing should be put over an old roof only if it is still even.

TILE OR SLATE
These materials last so long that it's unlikely you need to replace them unless the roof deck is showing signs of wear. If you have to replace them, have a professional do it.

METAL OR VINYL PANELS
Always remove panels before applying a new roof.

REMOVING AN OLD ROOF

If you have the time and money, it's best to remove the old roof for any job. If the existing roof is badly worn or uneven, you must remove it. Here's why.

■ The cushioning effect of the old roof under the new allows impacts from branches, hail, and even hard rain to dent the new shingles.

■ Any curled shingles or other flaws will show through to the new shingles.

■ When completed, there are usually telltale signs of the previous roof, such as curled shingles at the edge.

■ There is a limit to the number of layers—the weight of the roof—a house can bear.

■ The maximum number of layers may be mandated by local building codes.

ROOF CONDITION: Inspect your roof as described on page 8. If you find signs of leaking—moisture, stains, delaminating or separating plywood, or rot—remove the existing roof and repair the framing. Ice dams or splashing from the gutters often causes rot at the eaves. You can carefully strip off the first two or three courses of shingles, cut out the damage, and replace the removed shingles with similar new ones. This will give you an even surface for reroofing, but may take as much time and effort as stripping the whole roof, which would provide a better surface.

STRIPPING: There is no special trick to removing an old roof; it's just a lot of hard work.

Your best bet is to get a large bin from a waste disposal company and have it placed as close to the house as possible. Then throw the old roof directly into it as you work. Ask the refuse hauler about sizes, and don't get a container that will weigh so much it could crack your driveway. Lay scrap plywood under the bin. If a debris bin is not available, you can toss the trash into a pickup truck, which will probably get dented and scratched.

A common tool for removing shingles, roll roofing, or a built-up roof is a flat-bottomed spade. Home centers sometimes sell a shovel-like tool with a serrated end for roof removal. Another version of this tool has notches on the edge to help you pull nails. You'll also need a broad broom.

Start at the ridge. Break through a built-up roof at the ridge with hammer claws or a pick to get a starting point.

On wood shingle roofs, and sometimes on shake roofs, be sure to work your way from the top down so less debris falls through the openings. If you work at wood shingles and shakes from their bottom edges, the shingles themselves will help pry up nails.

A crowbar or pry bar also works on shakes and shingles. By running the flat end of the crowbar up under the shingles, then prying up, you can often remove a dozen or more shingles at a time.

Pick up tiles by hand, and pry up slate with a crowbar. To remove metal or vinyl panels, pry up the panels, pull the nails or remove the screws, then lift the panels off.

As you remove the roof, save the old pieces of flashing, particularly chimney flashings. They'll come in handy as patterns when you make new flashings.

Remove shingles with a spade or pitchfork, working from the ridge. Cemented composition shingles will sometimes roll off with your help (top). Remove the ridge shingles with a crowbar, as well as any shingles in tight spaces, such as around a chimney or in a valley. Sweep the roof regularly; loosened shingles and nails will make the roof slippery.

INSTALLING FLASHING

F lashings protect the roof where water could get under it, such as at joints in the roof, places where a vent pipe or chimney pokes through, valleys where two roof surfaces meet, or where a roof meets a wall. Some flashings are installed before the roofing goes on, others are put in place along with it. This section will help you determine what kind of flashings you need and when to install them.

KINDS OF FLASHINGS

Flashings are generally made of galvanized sheet metal, copper, or aluminum. Roll roofing serves as valley flashing on some roofs. And composition shingles can be woven together to form a valley in which no flashing is necessary—called a closed valley.

VALLEY FLASHINGS: Valley flashing is installed before the roofing material. The two types are open and closed. With open valley flashing, the roofing material ends a short distance from the center of the valley and the flashing material shows. Closed valleys are shingled across. The type you choose depends on the kind of roofing you use.

For metal roofing, use either the flashing designed to go with your roofing or W-metal flashing for ribbed steel. For roll roofing, flash an open valley with the roofing itself.

Open valley flashing works with any roofing material. Closed valley flashing can be done only with composition shingles, using either of two methods—fully laced or half laced. Some people prefer closed valleys because the roof has no breaks in color or texture.

For straight valleys between surfaces with equal slopes, an open valley with metal flashing

works best. If the roof has different slopes, weave composition shingles together to create a closed valley.

Metal flashing—called W-metal flashing— is often used with wood and composition shingles and wood shakes. Made from aluminum or galvanized steel, it comes in 10-foot lengths in widths of 16 to 24 inches. Use the wider type on lower sloped roofs, particularly where heavy rainfall occurs. Aluminum will not rust, but it dents, which can make it unsightly in hail-prone areas.

Valleys between a dormer roof and a main roof require flashing. Flash them according to the type of roofing and the roof slopes.

METAL OPEN VALLEY: Valley metal goes on after the roof and valley have been covered with underlayment (see page 38), if necessary. Lay the flashing in place, with its ridge centered up the valley. Trim the bottom edge even with the edge of the roof at the eaves, using tin snips.

Nail the flashing to the roof deck—placing the nails ½ inch in from the edge of the flashing—every 6 inches. Use aluminum nails with aluminum flashing.

If the valley is longer than one length of valley metal, start from the bottom and overlap the second length on top of the lower one by 6 to 12 inches. Seal the joint with roofing adhesive or rubber caulk. Trim the top flush with the top of the roof ridge.

While shingling along a W-metal valley flashing, snap chalk lines as trimming guides. At the top, mark 3 inches out from the center ridge on each side. Then measure the length of the flashing. Add ⅛ inch for every foot of valley length. An 8-foot-long valley would be 1 inch wider at the bottom than at the top. For a low-slope roof, add ¼ inch. Mark the bottom of the valley and then snap the chalk lines. If the valley is especially long, and the bottom marks are less than 6 inches from the outside edges of the flashing, move the marks in to 6 inches from the edge.

As each course arrives at the valley, the bottom corner of the last shingle tab must cross the chalk line. If it will fall just a little short, add a single tab into the course before the flashing. Avoid a seam between shingles on the flashing. Don't nail into the flashing; secure the shingle with an extra nail just outside the flashing.

When you have shingled to the ridge, find the original chalk line. You may have to carefully cut through the shingles at the top and bottom to find it. Then snap a new chalk line on the shingles, and cut them along that line. Lift the shingles and trim off the sharp corners, as shown on the opposite page. Cement together the

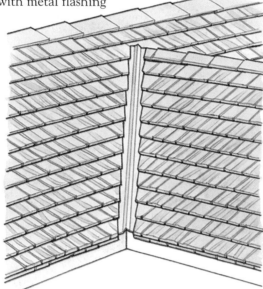

Valleys between two roof surfaces channel water. Flashing protects them. This open valley uses a W-metal flashing. Metal open flashings are commonly used for composition shingles and are required for wood shingles or shakes.

shingles that lie over the flashing with roofing adhesive.

ROLL ROOFING OPEN VALLEY: Mineral surface roll roofing can serve as flashing for an open valley. It's inexpensive, but other methods are more durable.

To flash a valley this way, cut a strip of 18-inch-wide roll roofing to the length of the valley. Center it—mineral surface down—in the valley, and nail it one side at a time. Snap a chalk line down the center of a 36-inch-wide strip of roll roofing. Center it—mineral surface up—in the valley, using the chalk line. Nail one side first then bend the strip to seat it securely in the valley and nail the other side.

Snap chalk lines 3 inches out from the center on each side, diverging ⅛ inch for each foot of descent as before. Cut the shingles on these lines when they overlap the flashing. Trim the corners, as shown below right, and cement each shingle edge to the valley and the other shingles.

HALF-LACE CLOSED VALLEY: A half-lace valley can be installed quickly, but it doesn't look as finished as an open W-metal valley or a full-lace valley. It works well when joining roofs of different slopes.

Lay the shingles from the lower-sloped roof across the valley at least 12 inches up the other side. Seams between shingles should be 10 inches away from the center on either side. If necessary, insert a one-tab shingle before reaching the valley.

Then lay the shingles from the steeper roof across to the center of the valley. Snap a chalk line 2 inches back from the center of the valley and trim the shingles along the line with tin snips to avoid cutting through the layers below. Trim all corners (see illustration at right), and cement them down.

FULL-LACE CLOSED VALLEY: The full-lace valley is more time-consuming than the half-lace because you lay shingles from both sides at once.

If the roof slopes on both sides of the valley are equal, the full-lace valley is a matter of crisscrossing one course under another as you work on the roof. As with the half-lace valley, carry the last shingle at least 12 inches up the other side, adding a single-tab shingle farther back along the course if necessary. Keep joints at least 10 inches away from the valley.

If the roof slopes are different, as in the illustration below, two courses of shingles on the flatter roof will cross to the other side before you bring one across from the steep slope. In extreme cases, it may be three to one. You will be able to tell which is necessary as you work. This is the reason a half-lace is a popular choice for roofs that have different pitches.

CLOSED VALLEYS

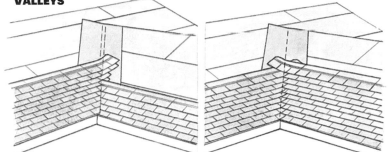

Shingles can be woven into valleys. For the full-lace closed valley (top right), lay the shingles in courses from both roofs at the same time, and overlap them in the valley. The half-lace closed valley (top left) is quicker because you install one roof surface first, then lay the other surface across it.

An open valley can be flashed with roll roofing. First lay an 18-inch strip of roll roofing, then center a 36-inch strip over the valley. Use a board to force the roofing into the bottom of the valley where it will be better supported by the deck below.

TRIM SHARP CORNERS!

Valley leaks are one of the most common roof leaks. They frequently result from a failure to trim, or dub, the sharp corners of shingles where they extend over the valleys.

Uncut corners can act as diverters during heavy runoff, sending water under the shingles until it drips into the house.

To dub the corners, lift each shingle in the valley and trim about 2 inches from the corner of the one underneath it, as shown at right. Then, raise the trimmed edge of the shingle and embed it in a 2-inch circle of roofing cement.

INSTALLING FLASHING
continued

VENT FLASHING: Flashing around vent pipes is straightforward with rubber-sleeved flashing. It is widely used with shake, composite, and wood shingles and roll roofing. Panel roofs require special treatment.

COMPOSITE AND WOOD SHINGLES AND SHAKES: The rubber-sleeved vent flashing is a flat piece of galvanized metal with a rubber collar that slips over the vent pipe. Select the sleeve based on the diameter of the vent, usually 1½ to 3 inches. Most furnace and water heater vents require all-metal vent flashings, which are installed the same way.

Before putting the sleeve over the vent, bring the shingles or shakes up to the bottom edge of the vent pipe. If the top shingle—wood or composite—hits the pipe, notch it to fit. If a course of composite shingles extends several inches past the pipe, cut a hole in a shingle and slip it over. For shakes or wood shingles, use a keyhole saw to notch the sides of two shingles so that they fit around the vent pipe. Apply roofing cement to the underside of the flashing's flat piece and slip the flashing over the pipe.

Nail it down lightly with a nail in each of the two upper corners—to keep it from sliding around. Then, lay a bead of caulk along the top and sides of the flat plate and cover the nail heads. Don't seal the bottom edge. If water does get under the flashing, it should have a way back out to the roof.

If using composite shingles, bring the next course across. Where a shingle meets the vent, cut the shingle in a smooth arc about 1 inch away from the edge of the rubber sleeve. Cutting it too close will allow debris to collect there and possibly dam up water. Glue the shingles that overlap the vent to the vent with a dollop the size of a quarter. Too much cement on composite shingles can cause them to blister in the hot sun.

For wood shingles or shakes, choose a broad shake or shingle—12 inches wide—to go above the vent. For a top-quality job, use a keyhole saw to cut an arc to fit the shingle or shake around the pipe. Or, you can saw the shingle short with a straight cut. Unless that top shingle or shake comes within ½ inch of the sleeve, don't just back it away from the pipe.

Don't forget that the lower edge of the flashing always sits on top of the course of shingles below it. This may not seem right at first, but you have to think of how water will flow down the roof.

Even the simplest roofs have vent and chimney pipes. The flashing for these is a simple, one-piece item.

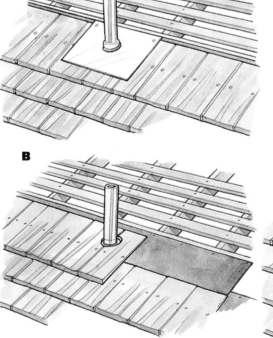

Like many flashing pieces, the vent flashing is installed between shingle courses [A, C]. Fit wood shingles around the pipe [B] then install the flashing. Fit the shingles in the next course around the flashing [C]. If the shingle directly behind the vent is far away, slide it down from its normal line to protect the back of the vent [D].

A

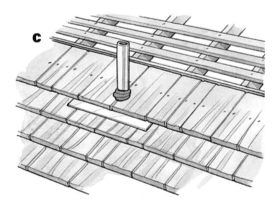

C

B

D

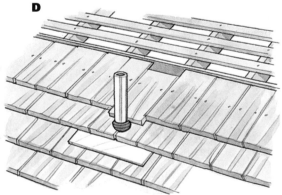

ROLL ROOFING

More precise cutting is involved when using roll roofing. Have someone help you to avoid tearing the roll roofing.

When you first approach the vent with the roll roofing, cut a hole just big enough to fit over the vent, then carefully place the roll roofing over it. Put the vent flashing over the vent. Draw an outline of the flashing on the roofing with chalk or a carpenter's pencil. Remove the flashing. Measure the length of the flashing from top to bottom with a tape measure. Split the distance to find the midpoint. The midpoint of 16-inch-long flashing would be at 8 inches. Measure that distance up from the bottom of the outline on the roll roofing along both sides. Use a straight edge to draw a line. Then, using a utility knife, cut along that line, extending it ½ inch beyond the outline on the roofing.

Next, measure the distance between the rubber sleeve and the edge of the flat panel on the flashing. Take measurements at the top and on both sides and subtract one inch. Measure in that distance from the outline on the roof. Using the measurements as guides, cut a semicircle above the midpoint line with a utility knife. This allows the roof to lie flat around the rubber sleeve.

Coat the bottom of the flashing plate with roof cement. Lift the roll roofing and slide the top of the flashing through the slit toward the semicircle that you cut. Let the bottom portion of the roofing sag away from the plate to avoid getting cement on the roofing. Carefully lower both the roofing and flashing together. The roll roofing should cover the top part and the lower half should be exposed. Then gently lift the roll roofing that now covers the flashing and cement it to the flashing. Put one nail through the roofing at the top corners of the flashing. Caulk any part of the midline cut that's exposed, run a caulk bead along the exposed side edges (not the bottom), and caulk over the two nail heads.

PANEL ROOFS

Use special panel roofing flashings such as Dekite brand flashing when installing. These special flashings have a pliable bottom plate made from soft 1-mm aluminum. This allows the flashing base to conform to the ribs or valleys in the roofing panel.

Begin by measuring where the vent pipe will come through the panel; cut a hole just large enough for the vent pipe. The more exact the hole, the less likelihood of leaking. Put the panel in place and attach it loosely so it doesn't move while you work on it. Put the

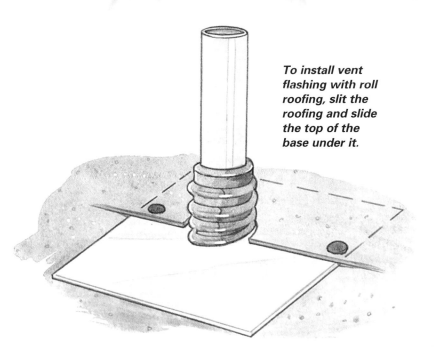

To install vent flashing with roll roofing, slit the roofing and slide the top of the base under it.

flashing over the vent pipe. Using your hands, the butt end of a padded hammer handle, and maybe a soft piece of pine scrap, mold the flashing's bottom plate to the roof panel's contour. It probably won't be a perfect fit unless you're at a flat portion of the panel.

Remove the flashing. If the panel hole is close enough to the vent pipe, seal the gap with caulk. If the gap is more than ⅜ inch, run a semicircular bead of caulk along the edge of the hole to serve as a water dam. Coat the bottom of the flashing with roofing cement and put in back in place. If the roofing panel sits flat on the roof, put one rubber-washer screw in each corner; otherwise use blind aluminum rivets. Run a bead of caulk all around the edge of the flashing and cover the screws or rivets with caulk. If you nail it down, use aluminum flashing nails.

If installing panel roofing, use flashings made by the panel manufacturer or a flashing with a soft metal base. The malleable base molds to the contours of the panel for a proper seal.

INSTALLING FLASHING
continued

If you can't find special panel flashing—or, as an inexpensive alternative for old-fashioned corrugated metal and fiberglass panels—you can just use caulk and, if necessary, caulking cord. Pack the opening in the roof and around the pipe with caulk. Spread the caulk above and around the pipe so that it rises in a smooth sweep from the roof and continues about 3 inches up the vent pipe. It's best to do this in layers of no more than ½ inch at a time.

CONTINUOUS FLASHING

This type of flashing is typically applied where the roof meets a vertical wall of a dormer or where a shed roof is attached to a wall. Plan—and adjust as necessary—the last three courses of roofing material before the vertical wall so that the final course, which will go over the flashing, will be at least 8 inches wide. Install the flashing before applying the last two courses.

Continuous flashing is a continuous strip of metal about 10 inches wide. You can buy it already bent or using a long, straight-edged board, bend your own from a roll of flat metal flashing. You will have to bend it to match the slope of the roof.

If the vertical wall has not yet been covered with siding, it's a simple job.

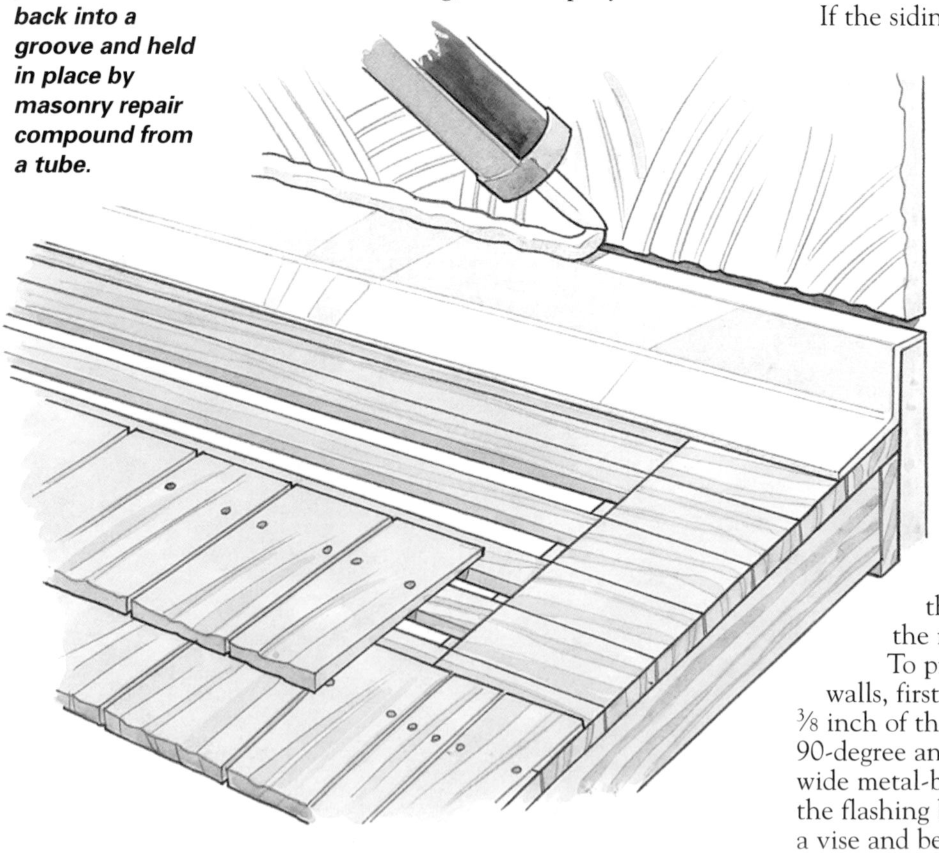

You need continuous flashing where a roof meets a vertical wall. For a stucco home, shown below, a long Z-shaped piece of metal is glued to the roof deck. The top part is forced back into a groove and held in place by masonry repair compound from a tube.

Slip the flashing under the felt or housewrap on the vertical wall, then embed the flashing on the roof in a layer of roofing cement. Nail down the flashing every 2 feet along the edge on the roof, but not on the vertical wall. This allows the house to settle without disturbing the flashing seal. (Use aluminum nails on aluminum flashing and galvanized nails on galvanized flashing.)

With the flashing in place, apply the final course of roofing material and cement, then nail it into place. Cover each nailhead with a dab of caulk. When you apply the siding on the vertical wall, don't nail through the flashing. Attach metal or vinyl siding J-molding to the flashed area with construction adhesive and as few nails as possible.

If the siding on the vertical wall is already in place, you must slip the flashing up under it. Gently pry the siding away from the wall and work the flashing up under it. If you run into nails, remove them or notch the flashing to fit around them.

If you're installing cedar shingles or shakes and the final course of roofing is too short for a neat appearance, there's another way to do it. Determine the angle between the roof and the wall. You can assume the wall is plumb and use the chart on page 22 (determining slope) to determine the roof angle. Using a table saw, bevel one edge of a clear cedar 1×4 board to this angle so it will fit tightly against the wall. Nail the board in place.

If the siding is stucco or brick, set the flashing into a groove in the rock-hard material. If a groove already exists from a previous roof, clean it out and reuse it. If no groove exists, snap a chalk line across the wall about 5 inches up from the roof. For stucco, install an inexpensive concrete cutting blade in your circular saw, and cut ½ inch deep into the wall for the flashing. You can chisel a groove with a concrete chisel and hammer, but work slowly and be careful not to crack the stucco.

On a brick wall, you can cut a groove, as above, or carefully chisel out the mortar between the bricks about 5 inches up from the roof.

To prepare the flashing for mortared walls, first bend the top ⅜ inch of the continuous flashing at a 90-degree angle. You can bend it with 4-inch wide metal-bending pliers or you can clamp the flashing between two boards placed in a vise and bend it with a block of wood and a

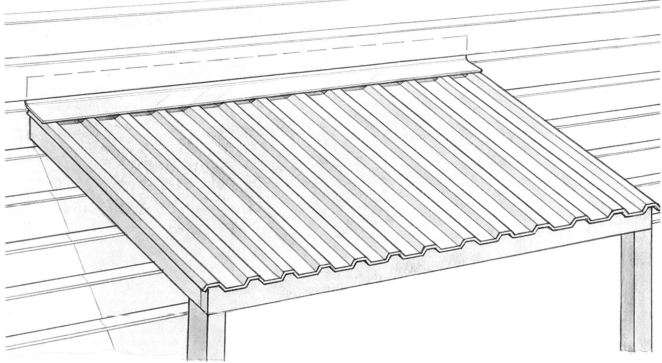

hammer. Next, bend the flashing horizontally near the middle so the lower half will fit evenly on the roof. Fill the groove with an exterior adhesive caulk and press the top edge of the flashing into place. Let the adhesive dry for at last an hour before finishing the job. Run a bead of clear silicon caulk on top of the flashing to seal the groove. Nail the last course of the roofing material over the flashing on the roof.

STEP FLASHING

Install step flashing where a vertical surface such as a skylight, chimney, or dormer meets a sloping roof. In this style of flashing, an L-shaped piece of metal goes under each course of shingles and onto the adjoining surface.

The process described here assumes use of composite shingles with a 5-inch exposure. The process is the same for wood shingles and shakes. For panel and roll roofing, apply a continuous flashing, as described previously.

You can buy precut metal shingles or cut them from flashing metal. They should be2 inches longer than the exposure. On a typical composite shingle roof with a 5-inch exposure, the metal shingles are 7 inches long. They should be about 10 inches wide. They'll be bent at a 90-degree angle in the middle, providing 5 inches of flashing for the wall and the roof.

To bend metal shingles, clamp one between two boards in a vise and hammer it over with a rubber mallet, as shown *below*. To apply step flashing, position the first piece on top of the starter shingle so the bottom edge of the flashing is flush with the bottom edge of the starter course. Nail the flashing to the roof with two nails, 1 inch from the top. Do not nail it to the wall.

To install continuous flashing on a wood-sided house, a V-shaped piece of metal must be inserted behind the siding. Sometimes this requires pulling the siding away from the house with a crowbar and then refitting it.

Bend step flashing from cut sheets of galvanized metal. Clamp them between two scraps of hardwood and pound them to a right angle using a rubber mallet.

INSTALLING FLASHING
continued

If the siding is already in place on your house, pry it away and slip the flashing up under it. Remove nails or cut notches in the flashing shingles to allow them to pass the siding nails. For brick or stucco houses, cap flashing must be applied over the step flashing as described in the following section. It's set into grooves and overlaps the step flashing.

Apply the first piece of flashing over the starter course. Next, lay the first course of shingles flush with the lower edge of the starter course. Measure and mark a line 5 inches up from the edge of the first shingle and apply the next piece of step flashing with the bottom end along this line. Nail the top. Then put the second course of shingles over it with a 5-inch exposure, which will cover up the metal shingle. If done correctly, the metal will not show. Continue up the roof.

FLASHING A CHIMNEY

This is the most difficult and important aspect of flashing a roof, because many leaks begin around chimneys. Although a careful homeowner can flash a chimney successfully,

Step flashing is installed at a wall or chimney before the abutting course of shingles goes on. Nail it only to the deck. If siding is in place, slide the flashing behind it.

call in a professional if you have any doubts. Begin flashing the chimney when the courses reach the chimney base.

Chimney flashing consists of a metal base flashing and a cap (or counter) flashing. The old chimney flashing pieces can serve as patterns for these pieces. The two flashing parts overlap but must not be joined together because the chimney and house settle at different rates.

It's best to construct a wooden cricket, or half-saddle—as shown in the illustration on the opposite page—to divert the water around the chimney. Otherwise, snow and water will build up behind the chimney and cause leaks. Make the cricket sides from ½-inch exterior plywood, nailing them to the roof deck to form a new short ridge. The cricket should extend to each edge of the chimney.

For a good seal, press each piece of flashing into roofing cement spread on the bricks. First, coat the bricks around the chimney base with brick sealant, preferably one that hardens rather than remains waxy or oily. Sealant helps roofing cement adhere to the porous bricks.

Now cut a piece of base flashing for the down side of the chimney, as illustrated on the next page, and bend it to fit around the chimney. You can make sharp bends by placing the metal between two boards clamped together or held in a vise. Embed the apron in cement on the roof and press the flanges into cement spread on the bricks. Drive a masonry nail through the flanges into the mortar joints.

Roof along the side of the chimney and apply step flashing, as described on page 35. Embed each piece of step flashing in roofing cement on the chimney side, and cement the end of each roofing shingle to the flashing. The last piece of step flashing may have to be cut and bent to fit neatly around the corner of the chimney.

Cut and bend a piece of flashing for the cricket, as illustrated. It must extend at least 6 inches up the back surface of the chimney. If the chimney is narrower than 2 feet, the flashing should also extend beyond the cricket and onto the roof by6 inches. Nail it to the roof.

If the cricket is wider than 2 feet, cover it with roofing shingles and let the flashing extend 6 to 8 inches onto the cricket. Then shingle the cricket, installing step flashing along the back of the chimney as you did on the chimney sides.

Finally, install the cap flashing. These pieces are set in mortar for better adhesion and stiffness. Mortar stands up to the heat carried by a chimney, too. Rather than mixing your own mortar, buy tubes of premixed mortar that can be applied with a caulking gun. (Some roofers prefer to put a high-temperature, exterior-grade adhesive caulk in the groove, on the brick just below the groove, and under the shingle.)

Set the flashing into the course of mortar, two bricks above where the base flashing stops on the chimney. Overlap the other flashing to within 1 inch of the roof. Clean and reuse existing grooves. Otherwise, pick out the mortar between the bricks to a depth of 1 inch with a narrow concrete chisel.

Install the first piece of cap flashing on the downslope side of the chimney. Cut and bend it to fit into the gap you've chiseled out. Cut enough pieces of cap flashing to cover the two sides. Wet the joint and pack it with mortar. Then insert the flashing in the center of the opening. Push it firmly into place. Press and smooth the mortar above the flashing with your finger. Work your way up the side of the chimney, letting each piece overlap the previous cap flashing by 3 inches. Bend the corner pieces to fit around the chimney on the topside. Cut and fit the cap flashing on the uphill side of the chimney so it works around the cricket.

Tie a rubber strip around the chimney to hold the cap flashing until the mortar dries. Mist the mortar with a bottle sprayer for two days to reduce cracking.

Flashing around a chimney requires flashing from below— step flashing— and flashing from above— cap flashing— which is attached to the chimney.

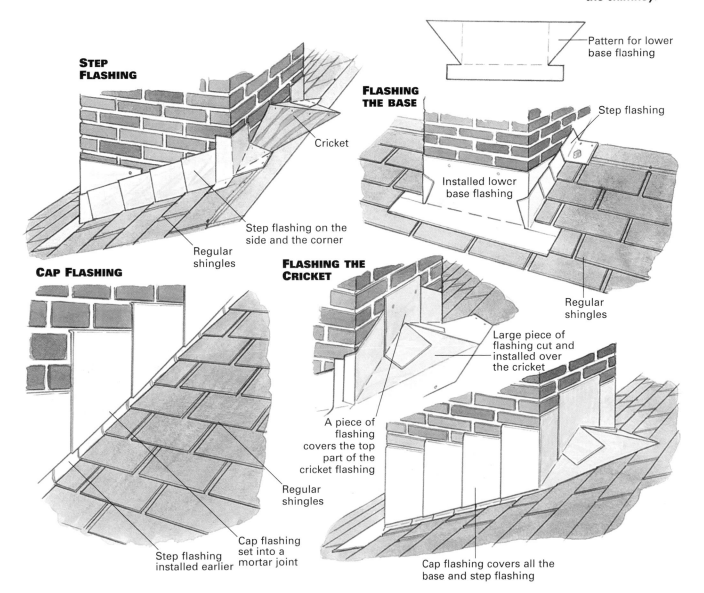

STEP FLASHING

Cricket

Step flashing on the side and the corner

Regular shingles

Pattern for lower base flashing

FLASHING THE BASE

Step flashing

Installed lower base flashing

Regular shingles

CAP FLASHING

Step flashing installed earlier

Cap flashing set into a mortar joint

FLASHING THE CRICKET

Large piece of flashing cut and installed over the cricket

A piece of flashing covers the top part of the cricket flashing

Regular shingles

Cap flashing covers all the base and step flashing

LOADING A ROOF

Stack eight or 11 bundles of shingles at the ridge as shown. This distributes the weight and keeps them out of your way until needed.

Be sure to have the roofing material delivered to the rooftop. Although wood shingle and shake bundles are light enough to carry up to the roof, a typical bundle of composition shingles weighs 80 pounds. That's a lot of weight to lug up a ladder and across a roof, particularly because you'll have to do it about 60 times.

Most lumberyards and home centers have hoists or conveyors to carry the roofing up. Conveyors are quick and usually allow the operator to deliver the bundles to different places on the roof for stacking. There is an extra charge for this service, but it's well worth it. Rent equipment if you have to.

If no conveyer or lift is available, set up two ladders so two people can carry a bundle between them in a sling or build a ramp to the roof wide enough to carry them up.

Stack the bundles of shingles or shakes on the roof in a way that distributes the load. Place them where they'll be out of the way until needed. The best place to stack them is at the ridge, because that's the last part of the roof to be shingled, and it's easier to slide bundles down than up.

To stack the bundles, place one bundle lengthwise beside the ridge, and another in the same position on the other side of the ridge, as shown above. Lay the next three bundles perpendicular across those two. Then lay the next three across those perpendicular to the first row. Add one more layer and then move 10 feet away and start another pile.

Try to get material delivered as close to project time as possible. Don't leave composition shingles outside in direct sunlight for long or the adhesive strips may glue the shingles together. Cover them with a light-colored tarp.

APPLYING UNDERLAYMENT

Underlayment is asphalt-impregnated paper, sometimes called tarpaper or roofing felt. It is described by its various weights per square. Roofers usually use 15-pound and 30-pound felts. It's cheap—about one-fifth the cost of the cheapest shingles you can buy—and offers a second layer of protection under your main roofing. Underlayment is not used in a roof-over, unless specified by a manufacturer.

The roofing manufacturer's instructions usually specify what type of underlayment is needed. For most composite shingle installations, one layer of 15-pound felt is usually enough. For shakes, see page 47 for a special technique to apply 30-pound felt. Manufacturers differ regarding underlayment for metal and vinyl panels and roll roofing. If the manufacturer does not expressly discourage it, cover the roof with underlayment. Wood shingles usually require no underlayment, but it is sometimes called for on a solid-deck roof under water-repellent shingles. Always check the roofing manufacturer's instructions.

The minimum overlap on the top edge—called a headlap—is 2 inches. You can have a larger overlap, but it will cost a little more in material. A 6-inch headlap will protect your home better.

Underlayment usually has printed white lines to align the layers. Don't use them for keeping shingles straight; there are two better methods described later in the section on installing shingles.

The felt must be laid flat and smooth or hot sun may cause it to buckle. To prevent this, tack it down and fasten it with a roofing stapler, which is swung like a hammer and sinks a staple every time it hits the roof. Don't put felt on a wet deck because the moisture will turn into steam that could blow a hole through the underlayment and eventually bubble and distort shingles.

Put two layers of underlayment on a low-pitched roof. Apply the first layer in the normal fashion, starting with a full-width piece (36 inches wide) along the edge of the roof. Overlap each layer by about 6 inches. Begin the next layer with an 18-inch-wide strip of underlayment. Overlap the layers by about 6 inches on this layer, too. This staggers the joints and reduces the likelihood of water getting into the house, even if the water backs up under the shingles.

In climates where snow can stay on the roof for even a few days each year, you should place a special ice barrier underlayment at the bottom edge of the roof. This underlayment is impregnated with an adhesive that binds it to the roof deck and to the next layer of underlayment. In cold climates, roofers used to paint the top and bottom of the first row of underlayment with roofing tar. Ice barrier underlayment is so easy to use, it's now recommended wherever melting snow could cause a problem. In warmer climates, you can start with regular underlayment. Glue the first headlap down with a bead of roofing adhesive to help protect against water backing up behind a pile of leaves.

To lay out underlayment, align it on one bottom corner of the roof and hold it in place with five or six staples. That will hold the paper but still allow you to straighten it. Roll the felt to the other side of the roof along the edge, pull it smooth and cut it flush with the rake edge. Tack it down with plenty of staples. Apply the next layer the same way, overlapping 6 inches at the headlap and about 12 inches on the sidelap.

When you reach the ridge, lay the paper across the top and tack it on the other side if you are not installing a ridge vent. If you are installing a ridge vent, cut it at the ridge vent opening. At valleys and hips, carry the felt at least 18 inches to the other side. Where a vertical wall meets the roof, such as around dormers, carry the felt up the vertical wall about 5 inches.

When you come to a plumbing or furnace vent pipe, roll the felt next to the pipe. Cut a slit in the felt where you think the pipe will fit and drop it over the pipe. Then cut the felt around the vent to make a good fit.

BURST YOUR BUBBLES

Small bubbles in underlayment—about the size of a dessert plate—happen. However, if there are any wrinkles or larger bubbles that you can't pull out, slit them from side to side with a knife. Then cut a piece of roofing felt as wide as the slit. Slide it up under the underlayment above the slit and let it overlap on top of the underlayment below the slit. Then tack it all down.

Proper underlayment installation ensures a waterproof roof. To work around vent pipes, roll the underlayment up to the pipe and mark where it will come through. Cut a horizontal slit, centered on that mark. Remove the flashing, slide the top part of the base up through the slit, then slide the vent flashing and underlayment over the pipe at the same time.

INSTALLING COMPOSITION SHINGLES

Applying a roof of composite shingles is more than a lot of nailing. It involves smooth underlayment, straight courses, and proper flashing and drip edges. This comes with practice. The secret to a good roof is careful workmanship.

The following directions are for a new deck or a freshly stripped deck (see page 26 for roof-overs). These methods apply to all roof shapes except hip roofs (see page 44 for shingling a hip roof).

DRIP EDGES

The first thing to install on a roof is the drip edge along the eaves. Drip edges are strips of painted steel that are nailed along the eaves and rakes of your house to prevent wood rot at the edges. There are two types: One is shaped like an L; but the newer type, shaped like a P, offers several advantages over the traditional drip edge. It looks nicer, protects wood better, and fits better over aluminum or vinyl fascia.

Nail the drip edge to the roof deck with steel nails. (If your drip edge is aluminum, use aluminum nails.) If your fascia is already in place, you can nail it to the fascia, too. Don't nail the bottom edge if fascia will come later.

After drip edges are applied to the eaves (not the rakes), lay the underlayment over the first section of the roof (see page 38). Drip edges for the rakes are applied over the underlayment.

FLASHING: The next step is to install the valley flashing, following the instructions on pages 30 and 31. Other flashing will be applied as the job progresses.

STARTER ROLL

A starter course layer is applied along the eaves for all types of shingles. Shingles depend on the layer below for adhesion, durability, and water protection. The first row needs an extra layer, too. This layer is applied after the drip edge, underlayment, and valley flashing are in place.

The easiest and cheapest way to install the first layer is to apply a starter roll. This is an 8-inch-wide, mineral-surface roll roofing that is nailed along the eaves and has adhesive for the next course. If you are not using a freeze barrier for the first course of underlayment, you should run a bead of roof cement to glue the starter course to the underlayment. (Freeze-barrier underlayment comes with its own adhesive.) The starter row should overhang the new-style drip edge by just 1/4 inch to reduce downward curling. For the old-style drip edge, the overhang is 1/2 inch. Then nail the starter roll about every foot just above its adhesive strip.

If you can't find a starter roll, you can use shingles as a starter course, but it will be at least twice as expensive and will take longer. The best way to use them is to cut the tabs

HOW TO MAKE A ROOFER'S JIG

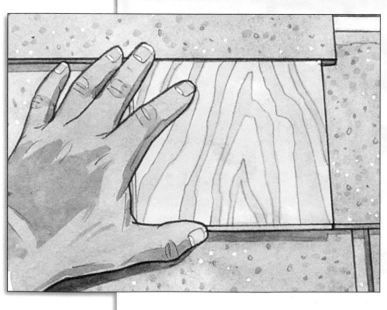

You can make a useful roofer's jig with just a few cuts on a table saw. Start with a scrap of 1/4-inch plywood or hardboard that has at least one original factory edge. Set the fence of the table saw 5 inches from the blade and run the scrap through the saw, keeping the factory edge against the fence. Then set the fence 6 inches from the blade and cut the 5-inch-wide strip into 6-inch-long pieces.

You can now use this jig to keep shingles straight when applying them in the popular 5-inch exposure. Also, when you need to cut 6 inches off a composite shingle for roofing in the common 6-inch horizontal pattern, this jig will show you where to cut. Finally, the 1/4-inch thickness gauges the correct amount of overhang for the starter course on the new drip edge.

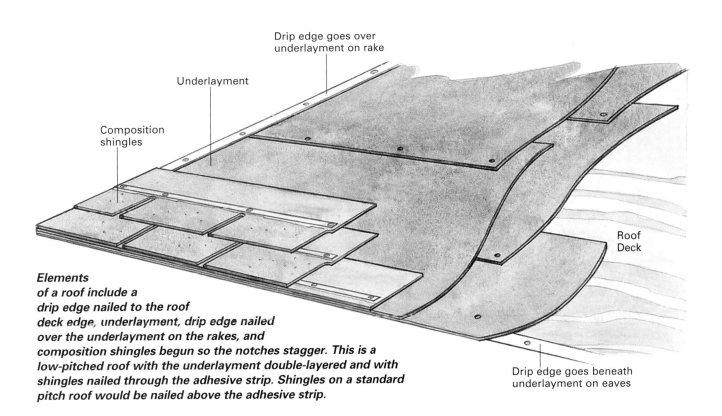

Drip edge goes over
underlayment on rake

Underlayment

Composition
shingles

Roof
Deck

Drip edge goes beneath
underlayment on eaves

*Elements
of a roof include a
drip edge nailed to the roof
deck edge, underlayment, drip edge nailed
over the underlayment on the rakes, and
composition shingles begun so the notches stagger. This is a
low-pitched roof with the underlayment double-layered and with
shingles nailed through the adhesive strip. Shingles on a standard
pitch roof would be nailed above the adhesive strip.*

from regular shingles. This method takes some time and the tabs are worthless scrap, but it puts the starter shingles' adhesive strips in the right place to secure the next course. Another trick is to reverse the first row of shingles so that the tabs point up the roof and the upper edge overhangs the eave. If you use this method, you'll have to add a 1-inch spot of roof cement under each tab of the next course.

NAILING THE NEXT COURSE

If you are right-handed, it will be more comfortable to start shingling from the lower left corner of the roof. Tuck your left leg under you and use your right leg to maintain your position on the roof. You will work up and to the right as you shingle. You'll probably want to reverse this order if you're left-handed.

Most composition shingles have three tabs. Each three-tab shingle is fastened with four roofing nails or staples—one nail an inch in from each end and one nail above each tab cut, just below the self-sealing adhesive strip.

It is important that the first course of shingles be perfectly straight. Make the overhang of the drip edge even. Measure the overhang or use the roofer's jig (see the box on the previous page). Then measure the

shingle, from top to bottom, and go to the other end of the roof. Subtract the overhang, measure up from the drip edge, and mark it. Now snap a chalk line and use it to align the top edge of the first course. On long roofs, measure once or twice in the middle. Pound in a nail just shy of the mark to help keep the line from bowing down.

To keep shingles straight, use the roofer's jig. Also, check for straightness every three or four courses by measuring up from the eaves at several places along the roof. Don't make the mistake of just measuring the ends, because the courses can bend and produce a roofwide bow. Snap chalk lines where the top edge of the next course will be if you think that will help you keep courses straight.

Shingles must be cut to fit around vents, at the rake, in valleys, and at walls and dormers. Composition shingles should be cut with a utility knife that has a special disposable hooked blade that will cut through the shingle in one quick stroke. A roofing hatchet also has a shingle cutter. However, the disposable blades work so well and are so cheap, even pros with shingling hatchets carry them.

START IN BACK

It's only natural to improve a little as the job goes on. So, start roofing on the part of your roof that's least visible from the street.

INSTALLING COMPOSITION SHINGLES

continued

SHINGLING PATTERNS

After the starter roll is nailed on, you are ready to start applying the shingles in one of two common patterns—6-inch or 5-inch. These terms refer to the distance each shingle is offset to the side from the one below it. A 4-inch pattern is sometimes used on low-pitch roofs to minimize the repetition of shingle seams. Shingles are staggered to prevent water from flowing through tab cuts. All patterns will protect the roof equally well.

SIX-INCH PATTERN: This is the easiest style to apply, so it's the most popular one. It's the one diagrammed in the directions on the shingle bundles (see page 38). Alternating rows start with whole tabs or half tabs. At the start of each course of shingles, you select a whole shingle or some part of a shingle, working in 6-inch increments. The remaining shingles in each course are whole ones until the last shingle. The resulting pattern aligns each cutout directly above another cutout in every other course. It's easy and works very well on most homes.

There is a problem with the 6-inch pattern on roofs that measure 40 feet or more from eave to ridge. It's difficult to keep the cutouts perfectly aligned up the roof because of inherent minor differences in the shingles. You can keep them straight, however, by periodically snapping vertical chalk lines as guides on the underlayment.

Start the 6-inch pattern by nailing a full-length shingle in the bottom left corner of the roof. Align the bottom edge of the shingle with the edge of the starter row. Place the left edge flush with the drip edge on the rake. Put another shingle at the opposite end of the roof and snap a chalk line between the two along the top edge to make a perfectly straight first course. Nail on the first course. For the next five courses, place the first shingle for each, then go back and complete the courses.

On the first shingle in the second course, cut 6 inches, or a half tab, off the left edge of a shingle. (Cut from the correct edge or you'll have a lot of scrap.) Many shingles are notched on the top edge at the midpoint of each tab to make this easier.

Use your roofer's jig to set the 5-inch exposure at both ends of the shingle, and nail down the shingle. Exposure is the amount of shingle that is left exposed when the next course is nailed over it. It's measured from the bottom edge of the shingle in one course to the bottom edge of the shingle in the next course up.

For the third course, remove 12 inches, or a full tab, from the first shingle and place the shingle flush with the rake. On the fourth course, cut a 36-inch shingle in half and begin with a half. Start the fifth course with the single tab left over from the third course, and begin shingling the sixth course with the half tab you cut off the first shingle in the second course. Ideally, you'll have half of a shingle left; that's large enough to use somewhere else, possibly for ridge shingles.

After nailing on the six starter shingles, carry each course far enough across the roof to allow you to repeat the starting pattern. Start the seventh course with a full shingle when the row below it is wide enough so the shingle will cover it, and repeat the process.

When you get to the ridge, fill out each course across the roof.

To keep the tab cuts aligned vertically, snap two chalk lines up the roof on the felt. Put the first one 36 inches in from the rake edge (the length of one shingle) and the second one 12 feet across the roof (the width of four shingles). If a dormer interrupts the roof, measure past the dormer to the first increment of 36 inches. Then snap a chalk line on the other side of the dormer to keep the pattern consistent. The process of working around a dormer is explained on page 44.

FIVE-INCH PATTERN: This pattern is widely used by professionals because it creates

The bottom roof shows the more standard 6-inch pattern, in which the shingle tabs align with those two rows above and below them. The 5-inch pattern, above, staggers the tabs so they don't appear to line up at all. The 5-inch pattern is particularly suited to large roofs.

a random pattern that helps hide imperfect alignment. The 5-inch increment is the same length as the shingle exposure.

In a 5-inch pattern, the first course begins with a full-length shingle. The second course begins with 5 inches removed from the left end of a whole shingle. There is a trick to doing this work quickly. After the first shingle is down, put the second-course shingle on top of it and then use the roofer's jig from the right to move it 5 inches to the left of the first shingle. Adjust the shingle for exposure and nail it down. Using a hooked roofer's utility knife blade, carefully trim the 5 inches off along the rake drip edge. This is all done without a ruler or tape measure.

The third course is installed in the same manner, offsetting it from the second course by another 5 inches. Always use a new whole shingle and save the parts for use elsewhere. Continue in this manner through the seventh course, from which you remove 30 inches. Taking 5 inches off the eighth course would leave only 1 inch of shingle, which is too little to work with. Start the eighth course with a full shingle.

Keep working up the roof, filling out each course enough to keep repeating the pattern up to the ridge. Cutting shingles along the rake is slow, but important. If done correctly, it gives you a very good base to continue across the roof.

When you reach the ridge, go back to the eaves and start filling out the courses, using

the roofer's jig to keep them relatively straight. Check your work every three or four courses to make sure it doesn't drift out of line. Do this by measuring from the bottom edge of the first course to the top of the most recent course at several points along the roof. The measurements should be the same. To help straighten out a drifting course, snap a chalk line. It's best to work out a drift over several courses rather than all at once. Only remove a course if it's badly out of line; no roof is perfect.

Start all composition shingle roofs with a full shingle, then reduce the width of the next courses by the pattern measurement (either 5 or 6 inches) until a new full shingle can follow.

NEW COMPOSITION SHINGLES OVER OLD

When covering an existing roof of composition shingles, it's best to match the shingling pattern used on the old roof.

The first step in roofing over an existing asphalt roof is to apply a starter strip along the eaves. Measure the shingle exposure on the existing roof (commonly 5 or 6 inches). If the existing shingle does not extend far enough out to spill water into the gutter, add enough to your measurement so the new ones will. Using whole new shingles, cut the tabs off. Then measure up from the newly trimmed edge to match the exposure in the old roof, plus any small addition to spill water into the gutter. Cut them again at this point. They should now fill the exposure and be level with the old second course. Nail them in place with the adhesive strip adjacent to the eaves. Cut enough starter shingles to go along all the eaves. Discard the tab ends.

On a 5-inch exposure roof, remove 2 inches from the top of shingles used for the next course and butt them up against the bottom of the old third course. This 10-inch

shingle covers the starter course and the second course on the old roof. Cut enough of these 10-inch-wide shingles to run the length of the eaves.

For a 6-inch exposure, lay a full shingle to cover the 6-inch-wide starter strip and the second course.

Now cut 5 or 6 inches—depending on the old roof's shingling pattern—off the rake side of the next shingle and butt it up against the bottom of the fourth course of existing shingles. This second course will leave a 3-inch exposure on the first course. This probably will not be noticeable. If you have a steep roof (where this course can easily be seen) trim 1 inch off the top of the second and third courses. This will give the first and second courses a 4-inch exposure, which will be less noticeable. With either of these methods that results in a shorter exposure, put a dab of cement under each shingle that sits on top of it. The second method requires more cutting and more cementing.

Cut and apply shingles for all remaining courses just as you would for a new roof.

INSTALLING COMPOSITION SHINGLES
continued

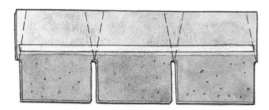

Finishing ridges and hips requires special shingles. You can cut them from a standard three-tab shingle as shown.

SHINGLING A HIP ROOF

Start in the lower left corner (or the opposite for lefties) and place the starter course and first course as you would on a standard roof, staggering the pattern and the seams.

Cut the shingle at the hip so it doesn't overlap on to the next section of roof. Too many layers at this joint will look uneven. Cut right in the middle of the hip, leaving less than ¼ inch between the shingles that meet at the hip. Start the second course in standard staggered fashion, cutting the shingle on the hip line.

HIP SHINGLES: Because ridge shingles cover the top of the last hip shingle, hip shingles go on first. You can buy hip shingles or cut your own from full shingles.

When cutting your own, cut the unexposed portion of the shingle slightly narrow so the edges won't show, as shown in the illustration below left. Place the first shingle at the eave and trim along the roof edge, flush with the starter strip. Then temporarily tack a hip shingle at the top as a guide. Snap a chalk line as a guide between the two shingles along one edge. Remove the top shingle. Apply the hip shingles from bottom to top, nailing each 1 inch from the edge just below the adhesive strip. Exposure for hip shingles is 5 inches.

Shingle the hips up to the ridge. Trim the last hip shingles so they meet evenly in the center of the ridge (see illustration). Slit a ridge shingle (same as a hip shingle) up the center of the tab about 4 inches from the bottom, and lay the top of the slit where the hip meets the ridge. Then bend over the half tabs and nail them down. Cover each exposed nail head with a dab of caulk.

RIDGE SHINGLES: Ridge shingles are usually attached with the exposed ends facing away from prevailing winds. For a hip roof, however, start from the hips and work toward the center. Put a shingle in place at each end of a ridge and snap a chalk line along one edge to align the shingles.

Lay the shingles with a 5-inch exposure and put nails 1 inch from the edges and just below the self-adhesive strip on the shingle.

At the center, trim the final shingles to fit. Then cap the joint with a shingle that has had the top portion trimmed off. Nail at each corner and cover the nail heads with caulk.

When shingling a ridge from one end to the other, trim and cap the last shingle the same way.

SHINGLING A DORMER ROOF

Shingle a dormer roof when the courses on the main roof reach the back edge of the dormer eaves. Shingle the dormer in a standard manner, using either a full-lace or a half-lace valley, as described on page 31.

Attach dormer ridge shingles—starting from the outer edge and working toward the main roof—before you carry the main roof shingles above the dormer ridge. When you get to the main roof, split the top of the last shingle and carry it at least 4 inches up the main roof. Lap the shingles coming across on

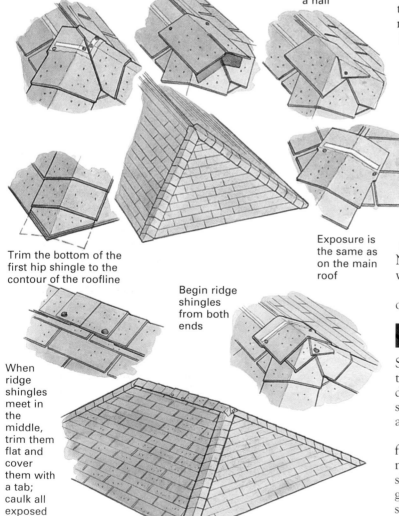

At the top, trim the shingles evenly where they meet so they don't bulge

Split the first ridge shingle about 4 inches

Fold the split ends and secure with a nail

Trim the bottom of the first hip shingle to the contour of the roofline

Exposure is the same as on the main roof

When ridge shingles meet in the middle, trim them flat and cover them with a tab; caulk all exposed nails

Begin ridge shingles from both ends

the main roof over the last shingle. Neatly trim the main roof shingles around the dormer ridge shingles.

TIE-INS: Tying-in a roof is a method of working around a dormer or other large interruption in a way that keeps the tab cuts vertically aligned and the shingle courses even on the sides and above the interruption.

To do this, shingle up the main roof toward the ridge, extending the courses toward the dormer. Carry the lower courses beyond the far dormer wall. Then build up courses along the far side of the dormer to the beginning of the dormer roof on the far side. Stagger tab cuts and shingle seams so they align with the shingles below them. Don't start a new stagger along the dormer wall. Take time to measure the exact shingle length.

As you reach the dormer roof on the left, shingle the dormer roof first. Then bring the main roof shingles over to it and complete the left-side valley, as described on pages 30 and 31.

For the tie-in, continue the course immediately in line with the dormer ridge to a point about four shingles beyond the right side of the dormer roof. Fasten these shingles with two nails at the top so the course that will be brought up to it can be slipped underneath.

Check the vertical alignment of the tab cuts between courses above the dormer and those below. Snap a chalk line between the top and bottom shingles beside the right eave of the dormer. Snap another line 36 inches to the right of it.

Follow these two guidelines as you lay the shingle courses up the right side of the dormer roof. Slip the tops of the last course under the tabs of the course you carried over the top of the dormer roof.

It's a good idea to snap horizontal lines across the roof on the right side of the dormer to keep that side aligned, too. Make any necessary horizontal adjustments over several courses rather than just one.

Tie in a dormer by shingling around it. Go across the bottom, up the near side, and across the top. Fill in the other side. Keep the courses even and the tab slots lined up.

ROOFING STEEP AND LOW-PITCHED SURFACES

If your roof has a pitch over 8 in 12, hire a professional roofer. On gambrel and some other roofs, however, you may be able to work on the low-pitch part and shingle the steeper part from a ladder or scaffold.

Low-pitch roofs once required tar and gravel or built-up composition roofs, neither of which are easy for a homeowner to do. Now, you can install

On a steep roof, put two nails above each tab, about 2 inches apart.

composition shingles on them by nailing through the adhesive strip on low-pitch roofs. (Shingles are usually nailed just above the tab cut, between the top of tab cut and the strip of adhesive.) Nailing through the adhesive hides the nail back a little, so water is less likely to reach it, and it seals the shaft and the head of the nail with adhesive to form a waterproof seal. (This gets the nailer tip of air tools gummy, so disconnect the hose and clean the tip frequently with mineral spirits.)

You can install roll and panel roofing on low-pitch roofs by following standard procedures. These methods are ideal for dormers, which often have low-pitch roofs.

Shingling steep roofs is more time consuming. Because the shingle's weight doesn't help hold it on the roof as much as on a shallower roof, you have to pound in more nails to prevent gravity from eventually tearing the shingle at the nailing spots. Use four nails per shingle on a regular roof; use six on a steep roof. On a regular roof, you would put one nail at each edge and one right above each tab cut. For a steep roof, nail the edge the same way, but drive in an additional nail about $1\frac{1}{2}$ inches to either side of each tab cut (see illustration). Also, you can't rely on gravity to help glue the shingles together so glue each shingle tab to the shingle below it with roofing adhesive.

INSTALLING WOOD SHAKES AND SHINGLES

Wood shakes and shingles are installed in much the same way, but each has a different look. Shakes look more rugged; shingles look more orderly. Shingles used to be so smooth they had to be installed over spaced sheathing boards to provide ventilation to prevent rot. Now, chemically treated shingles can go over solid sheathing. Shakes need an asphalt underlayment—installed under each course—to provide necessary waterproofing.

GENERAL GUIDELINES

Wood shakes and shingles are installed like composition shingles, with these differences:
■ The shingles are much narrower and require many more nails.
■ Wooden shingles and shakes are not uniform in width, so you must frequently try different shingles in a particular spot to find one that fits with a minimum amount of trimming.
■ Cutting wood shingles and shakes is difficult so you'll need a saber saw (electric jigsaw) or regular keyhole saw to cut around vent pipes and a circular saw to cut the angle for valleys.
■ In each course, shingles must be spaced from side to side with a gap between adjoining shingles to allow for expansion.
■ You can't cut hip and ridge shingles from regular shingles.

To establish a straight row for starting, install one shingle at each end of the eaves and run a line along the butt edge—the edge not lying on the roof.

■ Shakes require strips of underlayment, laid across their top edges.
■ You cannot install a new roof over existing shakes because they are too uneven.

Because cedar shingles lie together tightly, they can be applied on a roof with a minimum 3 in 12 pitch. Shakes work best when the pitch is at least 4 in 12.

Shingles and shakes usually come in three lengths for residential roofing—16, 18, and 24 inches. Shingles and shakes are also made in 15-inch lengths as starter shingles. Both shingles and shakes come in different qualities, but unless you're shingling a shed or other secondary building, there is no long-term economy in anything other than Grade No. 1 Premium.

Some communities and some insurance companies require that shakes and shingles be treated with a fire retardant. Even if it is not required, it's always recommended. Shakes and shingles should also have a preservative treatment to increase the life of the roof.

Each length of shingle or shake has a maximum exposure, regardless of roof pitch. You can install them with a shorter exposure to create a different look. You can use a roofer's jig (see page 40) or a roofer's hatchet to judge exposure.

Wood shingles are sawn on both sides. Shakes may be split (taper-split), sawn (taper-sawn), or split on one side and sawn on the other (hand-split and resawn).

A roofer's hatchet is handy for installing wood shingles and shakes—more so than for roofing with composition shingles. That's because this one tool will drive nails, split shingles or shakes to fit into spaces, and gauge shake or shingle exposure.

EXPOSURE CHART

Length	Exposure
16"	5"
18"	5½"
24"	7½"

TOUGH WOOD SHINGLES AND SHAKES ARE FRAGILE

Wood shingles and shakes can last a long time, but they are somewhat brittle. Nail them down with just two nails each. More nails just increase the likelihood of splitting. Once the shingle or shake is nailed down, don't try to push or tap it in any direction or you'll probably split it.

Metal drip edges are not used with wooden shingles and shakes. Instead, the first course of shingles overhangs the edge of the roof by 1½ inches.

Unlike composition shingles, wood shakes and shingles need a ¼-inch-wide gap, called a joint, between shingles to allow for expansion. Because the width of shakes and shingles varies, it's important to make sure that those joints are offset from the ones in the preceding course by 1½ inches. You may have to try several shingles, or split one, to find one that overlaps the shingle underneath by 1½ inches.

Nail down shingles and shakes with galvanized nails or aluminum staples from a pneumatic stapler. A shingle or shake, regardless of width, takes two galvanized nails, placed about ¾ inch to 1 inch in from each edge and about 1½ to 2 inches above the exposure. Installing shingles with a 5-inch exposure, for instance, calls for driving the nails through about 7 inches from the bottom edge of the shingle. The chart (below right) shows the minimum nail length for new roofs. Longer nails are needed for nailing shingles or shakes down over existing roofs.

A pneumatic stapler will make the job go more quickly. Staples must have a crown at least 7/16 inch wide and be the same length as the nails in the chart.

SHEATHING

Shakes and shingles are normally laid over spaced 1×4s, called spaced sheathing. This allows air circulation that helps keep the shingles from rotting. This method is required for untreated shingles. However, because the shakes' irregularities allow air to circulate under them, shakes can also be laid over solid sheathing, such as plywood, or over existing composition roofs. Shingles treated with a preservative can also be laid over solid sheathing. Solid sheathing should be used in areas that are prone to wind-driven snow.

The center-to-center distance of 1×4s for spaced sheathing should the same as the shake exposure. If you have a 7-inch exposure, nail the first board at the eaves to support the first course of shingles. The second and all succeeding 1×4s are then centered at 7 inches up from the eaves.

To speed up this process, nail on the first two courses of spaced sheathing. This first gap is not a normal one because the lowest board is not centered.

Wood shakes are layered with 18-inch strips of underlayment to provide a watertight barrier. The starter row and the first full course sit on top of a 36-inch piece of underlayment.

When you nail on the third course, the gap between it and the second course will remain constant up the roof—3½ inches in this example. Cut some scrap lumber that you can use as spacers so you don't have to measure each succeeding course of sheathing. Sheath the top 18 inches of the roof solidly so you can adjust the exposure to make the last course come out even at the ridge.

UNDERLAYMENT

A shake roof requires underlayment all the way up the roof. For shakes and shingles, especially in colder climates, you should also install an ice and water barrier at the eaves.

Underlayment is different for shakes than the underlayment shown earlier. For one thing, it's usually heavier—30-pound underlayment instead of 15-pound. And it's installed during the shingling process rather than before the shingling starts.

For this kind of roof, an 18-inch piece of roofing felt lays across the high end of the shakes on each course so it underlays the two next courses of shakes. (If you can't buy 18-inch-wide felt in your area, cut a full roll in half by cutting round and round it with a circular saw, using an old or cheap blade.)

SHAKE AND SHINGLE NAILS

Type of Shingle/Shake	Minimum Length
15", 16", or 18" shingles	1¼" (3d)
24" shingles	1½" (4d)
18" or 24" hand-split and resawn	2" (6d)
18" or 24" taper-sawn	2" (6d)
18" or 24" taper-split	1¾" (5d)

INSTALLING WOOD SHAKES AND SHINGLES
continued

Nail the top edge of this underlayment just enough to hold it straight; the subsequent courses of shakes secure it down.

The first strip of 18-inch felt is laid twice the exposure distance from the bottom edge of the starter course. So, if you are using 24-inch shakes with a 7-inch exposure, then the bottom edge of the first 18-inch strip of underlayment would be placed 14 inches from the edge of the eaves. Then the second course of shingles is applied. The bottom edge of each succeeding strip should be laid out 7 inches higher than the bottom edge of the previous one, overlapping all the way up. Lay the top pieces across the ridge. Weave the strips together at the hips to make overlapped joints.

When properly applied, the underlayment will not show on a completed roof.

ALIGNMENT

It is important to lay the first course of shingles or shakes straight. To align them, place the first shingle so it overhangs the edge of the roof deck by 1½ inches and the rake edge by about ⅜ inch. Place another shingle or shake the same way at the other end of the roof. Choose ones with straight, smooth sides along the rakes for a neat appearance.

Stretch a mason's line between the butts of the shingles, as shown in the illustration on page 46. Align the butts of the first-course shingles or shakes along the line.

To ensure that your courses remain straight, measure up from the butts of the shakes at each end of the roof—every three or four courses up—and snap a chalk line as a guideline for the next course.

Wood shakes and shingles come in varying widths. Leave a ¼-inch space between each one. Watch how the joints line up two courses up and down. A joint in one row should be at least 1½ inches from the joint above and below, and it shouldn't line up exactly with a joint two courses above or below.

APPLYING THE SHAKES OR SHINGLES

Space the shingles or shakes ¼ inch apart to allow for expansion. Drive in galvanized nails (see nail length chart on previous page) placed about 1 inch from each side and 2 inches higher than the exposure so they will be hidden by the succeeding course. The nails should penetrate at least ½ inch into the sheathing.

If a shingle or shake splits as you nail it down, just consider it two shakes and put a nail on each side of the split.

Apply the first course directly over the starter course. For shakes, there is no underlayment between the starter and first course. After the first course is applied, roll the underlayment out and lay it near the top of the shingle, twice the length of the exposure from the bottom. Tack it to the sheathing near the top of the underlayment.

Gauge the exposure with the roofing hatchet (see page 25). Because shingles and shakes are not uniform in width, you must constantly be aware of where the joint occurs. The joint between two shakes in one course should never be closer than 1½ inches to a joint below or above it. In addition, no joint between two shakes should be directly above another joint two courses below.

As you approach the ridge, lay out three or four courses temporarily and adjust them slightly so that the final course exposure will be comparable to the others. When you nail the final two courses at the ridge, the ends will extend above the ridge. Snap a chalk line flush with the ridge and cut all of the shakes at once with a circular saw.

VALLEYS

Flash the valleys with 20-inch-wide W-metal flashing. To keep shingles or shakes straight along the valleys, lay a 1×4 in the valley as a guide. Place one side of the board against the dividing ridge in the middle of the flashing. This will result in an ample 3½-inch space for runoff on both sides of the valley.

Shakes on the left side of the valley can be cut individually as you arrive at the end of each course, or you can precut all the valley shakes or shingles and make

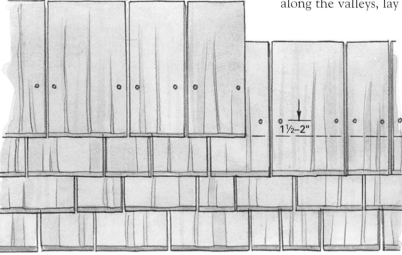

1½–2"

slight adjustments before you reach the valley. To cut them individually, lay the last shake or shingle at the valley over the 1×4, score a line across the shake and cut. To cut them in advance, find several wide shingles. Lay one over the 1×4, score it and cut it. Then use this one as a pattern for the remaining shakes and shingles. As you approach the valley, put a precut shingle up against the 1×4 and then find one or more shakes or shingles that will fit to the left of the valley shingle to fill in. You may have to split one of the fill-in shakes or shingles to get it to fit just right, but that's usually easier than cutting all the valley shingles individually.

The right side of the valley goes much faster because it is a starting point for courses. Position the 1×4 and lay out the bottom shake or shingle. Mark and cut, then, as before, use it as a pattern to cut all the other shakes or shingles that start a course.

HIPS AND RIDGES

Shakes and shingles for ridges and hips are factory-made to form a V. Each one has a seam in its crown; the seams must alternate going up the hip or across the ridge for maximum protection, as shown in the illustration below right. Nail hip and ridge shingles and shakes with nails long enough to penetrate the deck at least ½ inch—usually ½ inch longer than the nails used for the rest of the roof.

As with valleys, shakes or shingles running up the left side of a hip must be cut as you reach the hip. You can cut them individually or from a pattern, then fill in with shakes or shingles until they fit properly. If you cut them individually, use a straight board running up the hip to mark each shingle or shake. On the right side, cut the bottom shake or shingle at the proper angle and use it as a pattern to cut the rest.

When applying the ridge or hip shingles or shakes, guide your work by snapping a chalk line between the bottom one and one placed temporarily at the top. Apply a double hip shake or shingle at the eave. For a smooth fit, cut the starter one even with the bottom of the second course, as illustrated. Apply the first hip shingle or shake over that, and continue up the hip.

At the top, trim the inner edges of the hip shingles or shakes where they meet each other, then trim the tops flush with the ridge.

VENTS

When roofing around vents, carry the course to the vent pipe, then use a keyhole saw or saber saw to notch the edges for a close fit on each side. Slip the flashing over the pipe, then cut two layers of 30-pound felt to fit over the flashing and extend out a foot on each side, as shown. The shakes or shingles above the vent can be notched if they're too close. If they are too far away, one can be dropped down a few inches out of line to frame the vent. All the shingles or shakes should be about 1 inch from the vent pipe. Use broad shakes or shingles in such places to ensure adequate weatherproofing.

Next to a vertical wall, such as along a dormer, install step flashing as described on page 35.

To cut wood shingles or shakes for a valley (or a hip), lay a long piece of wood along the line to determine the angle of the valley to the butt of the shingles. Below: Alternate the position of the overlapping joint when installing hip and ridge shingles.

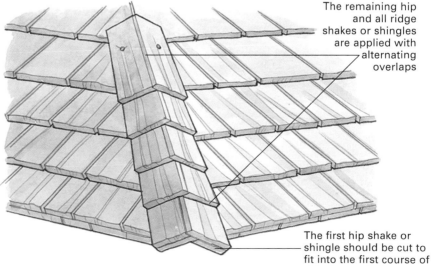

The remaining hip and all ridge shakes or shingles are applied with alternating overlaps

The first hip shake or shingle should be cut to fit into the first course of shingles or shakes

INSTALLING A PANEL ROOF

Modern steel panel roofs complement many home styles. Panels are best ordered precut (after careful measuring) to reduce the amount of cutting at installation time. Below, several companies make styled steel panels that look like tile or slate.

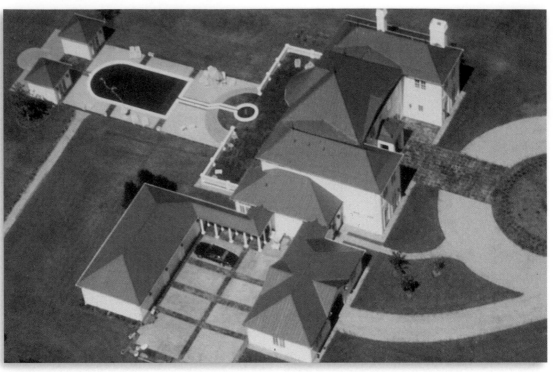

Painted and styled steel roofing has moved from the farm—where it is still the most popular roofing material for secondary buildings—into town. With modern choices, steel roofing provides a long-term solution for many buildings, and is the best choice for low-pitched roofs in most parts of the country. Fiberglass panels are widely used for greenhouses and patio covers. All are applied in a similar fashion.

GENERAL GUIDELINES

Panel roofs are relatively easy to install on simple roofs. But any roof that has numerous

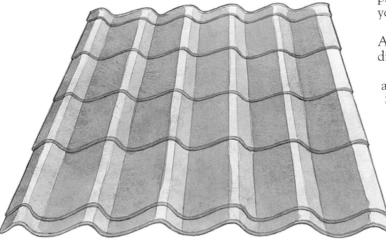

gables, varying roof angles, multiple pitches, or any other compounding factor should be left to a professional. This chapter covers roofing panel installation in standard precut sizes on simple gable-style roofs.

Metal roofs are not new—they have been used on buildings in Europe for centuries. However, except for secondary buildings, they are still not in common use in the United States, even with the major improvements in their appearance. Talk to a real-estate agent about how your local market will react to a metal roof. Even if a metal roof is right for you, it may make your home harder to sell.

All metal roofs can be noisy in hailstorms and rainstorms. Good insulation reduces this problem. Make sound insulation a part of your project.

The edges of metal panels can be sharp. Always wear gloves and don't let people work directly below you.

Metal and fiberglass panels can be cut with a special carbide steel blade in a circular saw. Special roller cutters work well on steel panels and can be rented. Small cuts can be made with aviation snips (compound-leverage tin snips). Be sure to wear safety goggles.

Panel roofing can be fastened to 1×4 sheathing strips or solid sheathing. Space the sheathing strips 2 feet on center. In areas where it snows heavily,

Steel roof accessories include ridge rolls and eave and rake pieces that give the roof a unified look.

the roof should have solid sheathing to support the load.

The best way to install panels is with special screws. These screws have a tip like a drill bit to drill its own hole. They also have self-tapping threads and a broad washerlike head with a rubber seal. Fasteners are always placed on top of a ridge in the panel rather than in a valley, where more water flows. Drive fasteners so that the washer is seated firmly against—but does not dent—the panel. Put a fastener about every 6 inches (depending on the pattern and the manufacturer's recommendation) from side to side, every 2 feet.

Panels come in 39- and 26-inch widths, so allow for some overlap; actual coverage is 36 or 24 inches. Most panels are custom-cut at the factory at little or no extra charge. Be sure your measurements are precise.

INSTALLING THE PANELS

Matching accessories for valleys, rakes, eaves, and ridges are available for most styles of roof

panels. They provide a better seal as well as a better look. The pieces for the eaves and ridges are usually installed first. The first panel is then placed at the bottom left corner of the roof. If there are no special accessories, allow a 2-inch overhang at the eaves and a 1-inch overhang at the rake. The first panel must be installed perfectly straight, because all others interlock and there is little room to make an adjustment in subsequent courses if the job starts out crooked.

When a roof requires more than one panel from eave to ridge, order long and short pieces and overlap them. The overlap should be about 12 inches, with longer laps—about 18 inches—on lower-pitch roofs. For added protection on low-pitch roofs, place a thick bead of caulk under the bottom edge of the overlapping panel.

Install the factory-supplied ridge caps to match your roof panel style. They overlap each other by 12 inches and are fastened to the roof like the panels.

INSTALLING ROLL ROOFING

Roll roofing comes in a variety of colors. It's a heavyweight composition roofing material that can be used on low-pitch roofs—down to a 1 in 12 slope with the concealed-nail method. This makes it useful on roofs where nothing else will work.

TEMPERATURE CONCERNS

Roll roofing can crack in cold weather, so don't apply it when it's below 45 degrees Fahrenheit. To finish a job after the weather turns cold, store the rolls in a warm area prior to application.

EXPOSED-NAIL APPLICATION

Apply roll roofing over a smooth deck, allowing a ½-inch overhang along the eaves. Cut it flush with the rake edges and nail on a metal drip edge with galvanized roofing nails, ¾ inch from the edge.

Cover valleys with 18-inch-wide strips of roll roofing. Nail one side every 6 inches. Completely seat the strip in the valley and nail the other side.

Snap a chalk line across the roof 35½ inches from the eaves to align the first course. Position the roll and nail it every 2 feet along the top. Put nails 3 inches apart at the rake and eave edges. If one sheet doesn't cover the roof, overlap the next piece by 6 inches. Nail the bottom section, apply roofing cement, then nail the overlap in place.

Snap a chalk line 34 inches from the top edge of the first strip as a guide for the next one. Tack the upper edge of the second strip. Then spread a 2-inch-wide layer of roofing cement along the upper edge of the first strip, and nail the second course over it.

If succeeding courses must be end-lapped, stagger the joints so that they are not directly above each other.

Cut the roofing to meet (but not overlap) at hips and ridges. Snap a chalk line on each side, 5½ inches from the center of the hip or ridge. Spread a 2-inch-wide layer of roofing cement from each line toward the center. Cut a 12-inch-wide strip of roofing to the length of the hip or ridge, gently bend it in the center to fit over the joint, and nail it down.

CONCEALED-NAIL APPLICATION

Roofing cement holds the roofing in place and makes it watertight with this method. Nails will not show when completed.

First, install valley flashing as described above. Then, cut 9-inch-wide strips and nail them along the rakes and eaves.

Snap a chalk line across the roof 35½ inches from the eaves. Lay the first strip along it. Nail the top edge only. Lift the bottom and side edges and coat the starter strips with roofing cement. Press the roofing down.

Lay the second course 4 inches down from the upper edge of the first strip. Nail it every 4 inches. Coat the overlap and rake starter with cement, and press the strip into place.

Make any end-laps 6 inches wide. Coat the bottom layer with cement, nail it down, then press the top strip into it. Cement the ridge strip into place and put weights (such as bricks) on it to hold it in place until the roofing cement dries. Cover the rakes with metal drip edging, cemented down and nailed every 6 inches. Caulk over the nail heads.

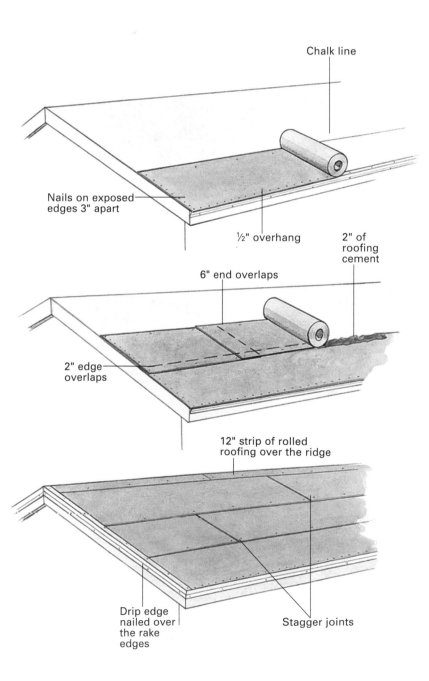

Chalk line

Nails on exposed edges 3" apart

½" overhang

2" of roofing cement

6" end overlaps

2" edge overlaps

12" strip of rolled roofing over the ridge

Drip edge nailed over the rake edges

Stagger joints

VENTILATING AN ATTIC

A properly vented attic will prolong the life of the roof, virtually eliminate leaks caused by ice dams, reduce cooling bills, and reduce moisture buildup in the attic that can lead to rot. It is one of the best low-cost improvements you can make to a home.

In a new home, attic ventilation is part of the insulation process. However, attic ventilation is relatively new; even homes built 20 years ago probably don't have all the proper elements in place. In some homes, attics are no longer accessible, so installing a new roof is your best opportunity to easily modernize your home.

First, take an inventory of what you have. The three major components of a well-ventilated attic are soffit vents, ventilation chutes, and attic vents. The soffit vents allow cooler air in. The ventilation chutes, installed between the rafters, make sure the cooler air gets past the insulation and keeps the air close to the roof deck. Finally, the attic vents allow warmer air out. The three parts work together to constantly draw cooler air in and exhaust warmer air out. This keeps the attic cool—or at least cooler. In climates where snow builds up on the roof, this prevents the home's escaped heat from melting snow from the roof up, which can back up under the shingles and leak into the attic. In all climates, ventilation keeps the attic drier.

The best system to install is a continuous soffit vent, ventilation chutes between the rafters, a continuous ridge vent, and square attic vents every 12 feet. By combining ridge vents with traditional attic vents, you provide ample ventilation that a ridge vent alone cannot always achieve.

At a minimum, install rectangular soffit vents, make sure attic insulation hasn't filled the gap between the rafters, and put in either square vents or a continuous ridge vent.

Rectangular soffit vents should be installed every 8 feet. A hole that is slightly smaller than the vent can be cut in the wood, vinyl, or metal soffit. Then the vent covers the hole and can be attached with screws into wood or rivets through metal or vinyl. Attic vents prevent insulation from blowing around and blocking the channel between the rafters, but if you can't get into your attic or you don't have much insulation,

keeping the channel open will have to suffice. A ridge vent ensures that the hottest air, at the top of the peak, has a way out.

Regular attic vents are easier to install. To install a regular attic vent in a stripped roof, slowly lower the blade of a circular saw through the roof deck to cut a 10-inch square hole 18 inches below the ridge between two rafters. On a roof-over, you'll first have to cut through the shingles with a utility knife before sawing the hole. The vent can sit on top of the old roof. It should be already installed when the course of shingles reaches that level. You can install a ridge vent on a house where a roof already exists or on a stripped roof. But it's difficult to cut through shingles and roof deck for the whole length of your house during a roof-over.

For correct attic ventilation, air must flow continuously. Warm attic air rises through the ridge vents, which draws cooler air in through the soffit vents. A vapor barrier below the insulation reduces moisture in the attic.

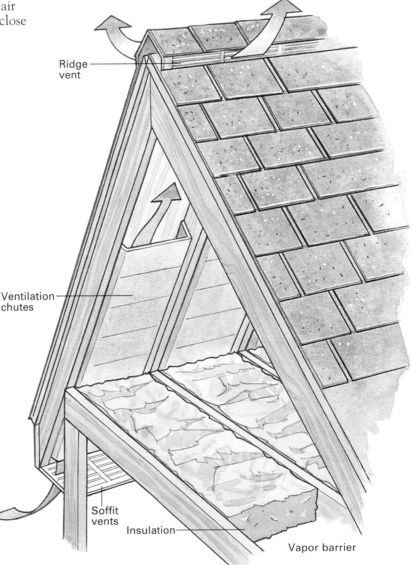

Ridge vent

Ventilation chutes

Soffit vents

Insulation

Vapor barrier

SIDING

Siding provides style and function. When you choose siding for your home, you need to consider not only practical matters like weather resistance, durability, and cost, but also aesthetics. Some style points to take into account include the architecture of the house, the neighborhood style, and your personal taste.

This chapter includes everything you'll need to know about selecting and installing siding, including preparing the walls and working around doors and windows. There are complete instructions for installing horizontal and vertical wood siding, aluminum and vinyl siding, plywood and hardboard panels, shingles, and some stucco lookalikes.

Siding is not inexpensive, but you can save 50 percent or more of the overall cost by installing it yourself. New siding that's carefully applied will enhance the appearance and value of your house.

CONSIDERATIONS WHEN CHOOSING SIDING

Siding material and color should reflect your taste and your home's style. Cost and ease of installation are certainly factors, too.

The style of your house might dictate your choice. A Georgian house might call for shiplap, a ranch house, vertical siding. A mission-style home almost demands stucco. The roof also may suggest a siding. For instance, stucco goes well with Spanish tile. You can often maintain the original look of a home while updating to modern materials.

Shingle courses align with the lower edges of the windows on this house— evidence of a superior siding job.

Your own taste and sense of style are important. If you believe that putting vinyl siding on your 200-year-old house would be like spray-painting graffiti on it, don't do it. But be careful not to rule out any type of siding without careful consideration. Prevailing neighborhood style is a factor to reckon with, too. You don't want to decrease the value of your home by making it the neighborhood oddball. Your home doesn't have to look like all the others on your block, but it should fit in.

In recent years maintenance—which means painting—has become a major issue. Most homeowners want siding that requires less attention.

Once you've settled on a material, you must select color, texture, and design; and there are many choices available. Manufacturers' brochures will show you the choices. They can also help you see what a particular siding will look like when installed on your home.

If you want to have the siding installed professionally, labor will be the largest part of the cost. Even inexpensive vinyl siding can easily cost over $150 per square (100 square feet) installed.

You often save more than half of the overall cost by doing it yourself. With inexpensive vinyl siding, you can save as much as 75 percent of the cost of the job. Most people find that installing their own siding saves enough money to make the time and effort worthwhile.

Among the less expensive materials are vinyl, hardboard, and composite wood panels, such as plywood and oriented strand board (OSB). High-priced sidings include redwood clapboard, stone, and fancy-cut wooden singles, such as those shaped like fish scales. Installation time varies little among different types of siding, so installing the most time-consuming kind rarely takes even twice as much time as the easiest.

To calculate the true cost of siding, you must include the long-term maintenance expense. With wood sidings, consider the need for regular painting (every 15 years) or staining (every 5 years). Aluminum, vinyl, and imitation stone require little maintenance. Stucco also is very durable.

A factor often overlooked by homeowners is the need for a solid surface for new siding. In most cases, the existing siding will be removed. If the existing siding is in bad condition or if it's aluminum or vinyl, it must be removed. If the home's current siding is 4×8 plywood paneling and it's in adequate condition, however, it should be left on to strengthen the house. Removing old solid wood siding and replacing it with vinyl could weaken a home's structure, requiring that you install new sheathing under the new siding.

Leaving the siding on any clapboard house makes an irregular surface, which can produce an uneven installation of new siding. You can level it out with thin insulation or furring strips, but then you'll need to extend window and door jambs and adjust other trim.

RELATIVE COSTS PER 100 SQ. FT.

Siding Material	Material Cost *	Est. Time
Inexpensive vinyl siding	1.0	4.6 hours
Stucco (professionally installed) @	1.0	6.8 hours
4×8 primed hardboard	1.25	3.3 hours
4×8 knotty plywood siding	1.25	3.3 hours
Troweled stucco substitute @	1.42	3.3 hours
12"×16' hardboard clapboard	1.5	4.6 hours
8"×16' prefinished OSB clapboard	1.67	4.6 hours
4×8 clear plywood siding	1.57	3.3 hours
Premium vinyl siding	1.75	4.8 hours
4×8 fiber cement panels	1.8	4.6 hours
4×8 T-111 grooved plywood	1.87	3.3 hours
4×8 prefinished OSD panel	1.95	3.3 hours
8"×16' fiber cement clapboard	2.15	5.5 hours
Hollow aluminum siding	2.52	4.8 hours
Prefinished premium hardboard	2.6	4.8 hours
Premium vertical vinyl siding	2.6	4.8 hours
Cedar shakes	2.65	6.0 hours
1×4 beaded vertical pine	3.0	3.6 hours
Primed cedar shingles	3.25	3.6 hours
8" cedar clapboard	3.3	3.6 hours
Insulation-core aluminum siding	3.32	4.8 hours
Steel siding	3.5	6.8 hours
1×6 spruce or pine car siding	3.6	3.6 hours
2×6 spruce	4.75	3.6 hours
2×8 log-look siding	5.15	4.0 hours
Imitation (cast) stone	8.25	12 hours
Fancy-cut scalloped shingles	9.0	6.0 hours
Remove old siding	N/A	0.5 hour
Stain#	$5	1.2 hours
Paint#	$20	2.1 hours

Doesn't include insulation, except where noted, or fasteners, trim, soffit, and fascia, which change from house to house. This is estimated by taking the professional rate and multiplying by 1.5 and includes time in a typical day not spent on the task. # Paint (2 coats prime and 2 coats finish) or exterior wood stain is required on all wood surfaces; however, some materials are prefinished or preprimed where noted. @ Doesn't include appropriate sheathing. For reference only; not recommended as a do-it-yourself project.

Overview of Types Of Materials

Siding is manufactured from a wide range of materials. Here is a survey of popular siding materials, fasteners, and finishes.

WOOD

In all its forms and with all its choices, wood siding still remains a popular choice for residential siding. Wood siding is solid lumber or composite lumber, such as plywood or hardboard. And it comes in different shapes and sizes, including panels and horizontal strips. All wood—unless treated with a fire retardant—is combustible.

SOLID WOOD: Milled from lumber, these are boards—often with special edges or profiles—or shingles or shakes. If made from cedar or redwood, or treated with a preservative, it can last 50 years or more. It requires painting or staining.

PLYWOOD: Although plywood has its detractors, it is a durable and extremely strong building material. After solid wood, it is the next most durable. As its name implies, it is made of layers of wood glued together. All plywood siding must be exterior grade and can be stained or painted. Plywood siding styles include smooth and rough finishes; grooved panels imitate board siding.

ORIENTED STRAND BOARD (OSB): This is not as strong or durable as plywood, but it has become a mainstay of building materials. It has the advantage of being molded so OSB clapboard siding can have a wood-grain appearance. It ordinarily comes factory-primed and must be reprimed and painted after installation.

HARDBOARD: This is the least expensive of the exterior-grade composite sidings. It is made of heat-processed wood pulp pressed into sheets. Although recent improvements have made it last longer, it's usually the choice of low-cost housing. It must be primed, painted, and repainted regularly or it will deteriorate. Hardboard siding is produced as panels or horizontal strips in a wide variety of styles, ranging from a stucco look to embossed sheets that resemble shingles.

SHINGLES AND SHAKES

Cedar shakes or shingles are long-standing favorites for siding. Their relatively high cost is offset by several factors: You can install them yourself, they're attractive, they don't need painting or staining (although you can do either), and they will last for many years. Both are sold unfinished or preprimed. Also available are 4×8-foot panels with real wood shingles already attached. These panels are installed like panel siding but give the look of regular shingles.

Redwood siding combines great looks with durability. Suited to a natural finish (as above) or painting, it comes in a variety of horizontal and vertical patterns to match many architectural styles.

Shingles are not difficult to install, but the job takes time. Panelized shingle siding is installed more quickly and looks the same. Shingles require periodic maintenance. Panelized shingles need less.

Two types of cedar shingles are commonly used: red cedar, which weathers to a silvery gray or medium brown, depending on local climate; and white cedar, which weathers to a silvery gray. All shingles should be treated with a wood preservative. You can either buy treated shingles—which is recommended—or apply preservative after installation. Shingles also come pretreated with a fire retardant.

Shingles come in grades 1, 2, and 3. Grade 2 is adequate for siding. Fancy-cut shingles, which allow you to create a variety of patterns, are usually made from more expensive grade 1 shingles.

You can get the shingle look for less money with vinyl shingles. These come in panels of 12 shingles and are applied like vinyl siding.

FIBER CEMENT

Fibers strengthen this long-lasting cement product without adding much weight. Even without paint, this siding will outlast its owner. Because it's made with concrete, it requires special tools to cut and it must be drilled before nailing. It takes longer to install than most other products. Despite its longevity, it can be brittle. It's generally available as horizontal siding boards or in 4-foot-wide panels, either 8, 9, or 10 feet tall.

METAL SIDINGS

Steel and aluminum siding are popular. Metal siding comes in various widths to replicate traditional clapboard siding. Metal sidings used to be finished with baked-on enamel but now have a thin coating of vinyl instead. This provides the long-lasting, chip-resistant color of vinyl while retaining the metal's rigidity.

The chief advantages of aluminum siding are its long life, wide range of colors and textures, and relatively low maintenance. Although fireproof, aluminum itself is a poor heat insulator, so it often is applied over sheets of rigid insulation, which also reduces noise during rain and hailstorms. Because aluminum is an electrical conductor, some local codes may require electrical grounding of the siding.

Cheaper metal varieties dent easily. Dents will give siding a pockmarked appearance and in some cases may break the enamel coating. However, individual panels can be replaced. In some climates, an enamel finish will eventually chalk and fade.

Steel siding continues to grow in popularity as a residential siding. It resists dents better than aluminum, making it a popular choice in the hail-prone regions of the country. Like aluminum, it is fireproof. It is not a good choice in areas near saltwater or where there

is heavy air pollution because cut edges (around doors and windows) will rust. Any scratches in the finish must be touched up promptly. Steel siding is installed in the same manner as aluminum siding, but it's more difficult to cut and it's heavier, so you may want to have it professionally installed.

Fiber cement siding requires careful installation. Once installed, it lasts a long time with little or no maintenance. It is available in several colors or you can paint it.

Steel (shown) and aluminum sidings are durable and require minimal maintenance. Aluminum siding is easier than steel to cut and install, so it is often the choice for do-it-yourselfers.

OVERVIEW OF TYPES OF MATERIALS
continued

Vinyl siding comes in many quality grades and styles. It's a good choice for do-it-yourself installation.

VINYL

Vinyl siding has come of age. It is now the most popular siding material in the country. The reasons are simple: It's durable, inexpensive, attractive, and perhaps the easiest siding for the do-it-yourselfer to install.

It is available in designs to go with virtually any style. Even some historic homes have been clad in vinyl without losing their period look. Vinyl is installed in much the same way as metal and has a similar appearance when completed. Being a plastic, vinyl is more flexible and easier to work with than metal (especially during warm weather), but precise cutting and fitting is still needed. Vinyl has a high resistance to dents and transmits less wind noise than aluminum. Because the color is uniform throughout the panel, rather than just on the surface, it is does not chip. It can be cleaned easily with soap and water. Some vinyl manufacturers make siding with insulated backing or design it to be applied with drop-in insulation panels. Cracked or broken panels can be easily replaced.

However, vinyl does have its drawbacks. Uneven sheathing shows through vinyl more than with other types of siding. Vinyl expands and contracts, so it can buckle if installed too loosely or too tightly. Certain colors, especially dark ones, are more subject to fading (red can eventually become pink). It can break if something strikes it when it's very cold. Vinyl is not fireproof, but it won't add fuel to a fire.

STUCCO

One of the most durable sidings available for houses, stucco is made of portland cement, lime, building sand, and water. It is applied in three separate coats, with the desired color of pigment mixed into the finish coat so no painting is required. Applying it yourself will cut costs by more than 50 percent, but don't attempt it if you don't know how. It is physically difficult to apply and can crack if applied incorrectly or if the house settles enough. Hire a professional installer for all major projects.

There are several stucco substitutes. Most of these come premixed in large pails and are applied with a trowel. A texture can be added with a special roller or trowel. These are one-step or two-step processes and don't require as much work.

Stucco provides a durable exterior surface. It suits Spanish and southwestern architectural styles and adapts well to others.

MASONRY

Masonry sidings include brick, stone, and imitation brick and stone. This book only touches on the installation of brick and stone veneers for prominent features; they are mentioned because they can be installed as accents to make your siding job unique. For instance, split imitation fieldstone over a porch wall might improve the looks of your home at reasonable cost. It's best to have these installed by a contractor who works with the materials regularly.

Brick or stone masonry can lend a substantive air to a house. Masonry often accents other types of siding.

FASTENERS

Ring-shank or specialty siding nails should be used to install siding. Some specialized siding nails resemble finishing nails, but using actual finishing nails will cut longevity. All nails should be corrosion resistant—stainless steel, galvanized, or aluminum. Except for shingles and shakes, you want the nails to go into the wall studs.

When installing wood siding, use 1-inch or longer box nails for shingles and 2-inch or longer ones for shakes. Galvanized nails are best for wood; they resist rust and their rough coating grabs the wood better. If aluminum or stainless steel nails are used, they should be ribbed for better adhesion. Avoid cheap galvanized nails; if the coating fails, the heads will rust and stain the siding.

If new siding is installed over old, the nails must penetrate the studs by at least 1 inch—preferably 1½ inches.

Sometimes nails can be purchased that match the color of prefinished siding, such as prefinished hardboard. Combining colored nails with matching caulking compound can save time finishing the job.

Aluminum, stainless-steel, or other corrosion-resistant box or roofing nails should be used with aluminum or vinyl siding. Nailheads should be a minimum of ⁵⁄₁₆ inch, with ⅛-inch diameter shanks. When installing steel siding, use galvanized steel nails to avoid corrosion that can result from the contact of dissimilar metals.

PROTECTIVE COATINGS

A properly applied exterior finish enhances the look of wood siding and, more importantly, protects it from the elements. Wood siding can be stained, painted, or treated with a clear preservative for natural color. Metal and vinyl sidings come with a factory-applied finish. Along with masonry and stucco, they can be painted for color, but usually don't need added protection.

Water is wood's main enemy; sunlight is the second. Most finishes protect well against water. Coatings with more pigment or UV inhibitors can protect against sun. Semi-transparent stains don't protect as well as opaque stains, and a natural finish does not protect against the sun, unless the finishes specifically offer UV protection.

Siding manufacturers recommend coatings best suited for their products and often provide instructions for proper application.

PAINTS

Oil-base and latex house paints and exterior enamels are available in a wide variety of colors. Oil-base paint was once considered the most durable, but many of today's latex house paints offer 20-year warranties.

Paints have three components: pigment, binders, and vehicle. The pigment gives paint its color. Binders help it adhere to surfaces. The vehicle is the liquid that carries them.

Primers are paints with high binder content. They adhere well to surfaces and provide a base for the top-coat paint, which provides the color and protection. Many painters prefer to apply oil-base primer and a latex top coat.

Always prime new wood siding before painting. This is especially important on the south and west sides of the house because they weather more rapidly. Make sure the primer you use on cedar or redwood is compatible with the natural acids in the wood. Most primers for cedar and redwood are oil-base.

WOOD STAINS

Stains enhance the natural appearance of wood and often contain mildew and rot inhibitors with water-repellent additives. The best stains penetrate the wood.

Penetrating stains are available as transparent, semitransparent, or opaque. Transparent stains protect the wood, add a hint of color, and slow the gradual process of color change. Semitransparent stains contain pigment, which makes them more durable than transparent stains. However, the pigment changes the color of the wood more and can change such characteristics as grain and knots. Opaque stains contain more pigment, so they hide the color and grain of the wood but have no effect on its surface texture. They do not penetrate the wood as well as the other stains, and act more like thin paint.

WOOD PRESERVATIVES

A clear water-repellent sealer will maintain the natural look of red cedar, redwood, and cypress. This has the added advantage of preventing unwanted stains. It may darken the wood, and must be reapplied every year or two—a relatively easy process that usually can be done in a day.

Paint and stain aren't for appearance only; they help protect wood siding from the weather.

ESTIMATING AND ORDERING MATERIALS

To assess material needs, draw your home, note all the measurements, and show the sketch to the lumber dealer to get the correct amount. You'll probably need to calculate square footage of the walls to compare costs between materials.

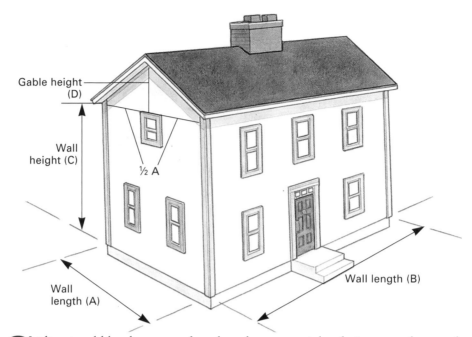

Gable height (D)

Wall height (C)

½ A

Wall length (A)

Wall length (B)

Siding is sold by the square foot, board foot, or square (100 square feet of coverage), depending on the material. In order to know how much to order (and what your project will cost), you need to determine the surface area of your exterior walls.

ESTIMATING TECHNIQUES

To estimate how much siding you'll need, first calculate the house's total surface area. The easiest way to do this accurately is to divide the surfaces into rectangles and triangles.

Measure the height (C, in the illustration) and width of each wall of the house (A and B shown). Multiply length times width for each wall to determine its area in square feet. Figure each gable end as a triangle, with a height of D and a base length of ½A. The area of each triangle is ½×base length×height.

Add all of your figures together. You should include windows and doors to allow for waste, unless your home has a lot of large windows. Cutting for gable ends creates waste, so add 10 percent to the gable area. It's best to have siding left over to use for repairs later.

For vinyl or metal siding, measure the total length around the base of the house to determine the number of starter strips. Also measure for other trim and accessories. Add 10 percent to the total to allow for waste.

BUYING SIDING

Most dealers will calculate how much siding you need based on your figures. If you are special ordering a product, make sure you show your figures to the retailer so you don't run short.

Shakes and shingles are priced by the square and come in several bundles per square. Wood clapboard siding is sold by the linear foot.

Plywood and hardboard panels are sold by the sheet, like plywood. It's best to buy a length that will cover from soffit to foundation without seams. Two-story homes will need at least two courses of panels of a length to minimize seams.

Aluminum, vinyl, and steel siding are usually sold by the two-square carton. Trim pieces, however, are sold by the linear foot. If you are buying siding for an entire house, ask about a price discount.

DELIVERY AND STORAGE

Because of the bulk and weight of most siding products—strips are as long as 16 feet—it's best to have your siding delivered. If you haul it, make several trips to lighten the loads.

The best place to store siding is in your garage. This keeps it out of the elements and, by closing the door, out of the neighbors' sight. If storing materials on a lawn, place 2×4s on the ground every 2 feet to protect the materials from the lawn moisture. Cover the materials with a tarp. Don't stack vinyl or metal siding higher than 4 feet.

Avoid handling the siding any more than necessary. Once installed, it's quite durable, but careless handling before can break vinyl, crease aluminum, and scratch wood.

DEALING WITH EXISTING SIDING

Like many remodeling projects, getting ready to install new siding on your house can be a project by itself.

REMOVE IT OR LEAVE IT

Base the decision of whether to remove the existing siding on the following factors:

CONDITION: Rotting siding harbors insects.

SMOOTHNESS: An uneven surface will make the new siding look wavy.

SHEATHING: If your home is sheathed in soft reconstituted wood sheathing—the black, bulletin-board-type material you may have to replace it with plywood or brace the wall studs if you remove the existing siding.

WINDOW AND DOOR DEPTH: The time you would spend adding extensions to door and window jambs may be more than what it would take to remove old siding.

The best decision is usually to remove the siding, but there are exceptions.

If your home is sided with plywood panels, it's possible the siding is doing double duty—protecting against the elements and adding to the structural integrity of the home. Try prying up a corner enough to see if there is anything else behind it. In most cases, unless a house has already been re-sided once, leaving plywood paneling in place is easier than trying to remove it, as long as the next layer of siding doesn't require extra time and effort on door and window extensions.

Removing stucco is never recommended. If your home has stucco now, either have professionals add a new layer or use a stucco substitute. Any other siding will require extensive drilling and furring to attach.

If your current siding contributes to the structural integrity of your house but needs to be replaced because it is rotten, you may have to install plywood or oriented strand board sheathing before the new siding goes on.

Removing old siding is straightforward. Using a prybar or crowbar, begin in one top corner and start prying it off. If you need a fulcrum for the crowbar, use a scrap of 1×3 so you don't poke holes in the sheathing. It's best to arrange in advance to have a refuse bin positioned near the house so you can place the old siding in it directly.

Whether you leave or remove the old siding, you will need to remove all shutters, downspouts, lights, outdoor shades, trellises, and other decorative fixtures before installing your new siding.

You can leave old siding in place—even if it has bubbled paint and cracks—as long as it will make a smooth-enough surface. Nail down warped pieces and replace missing ones to provide a good base for the new siding.

DEFEATING TERMITES

Termites are antlike creatures that eat and live in wood. An infestation can destroy a home. Termites often build mud tunnels up from the ground along the foundation to reach the wood portions of your home. The best way to combat them is to put a metal barrier in their way—either a special metal termite flashing or adding metal flashing to the bottom of wood siding. A simple L-shaped metal flashing that sticks out about 1½ inches from the home is usually enough. Use treated lumber if termites are known to be in your area. The preservative in the wood makes it less appealing to termites.

PREPARATION FOR INSTALLATION

Preparations will depend on whether you are installing siding on new construction or over existing siding. It will also depend on the type of siding you install. New construction will require sheathing. You should wrap your home to reduce air infiltration, and adding insulation can only help.

House wrap over the sheathing cuts down air infiltration..

INSTALLING SHEATHING

If you are replacing solid wood siding with less rigid sidings such as vinyl, you may need to replace or improve the wall sheathing. This could affect your home's structural integrity, so check your local building code.

Sheathing provides a solid base for installing new siding and adds rigidity to the walls.

Exterior CDX grade plywood makes the best sheathing; it's strong and durable. It's also the most expensive. Fiberboard or oriented strand board (OSB) designed for exterior use can be used as sheathing. Corners should always be sheathed with plywood.

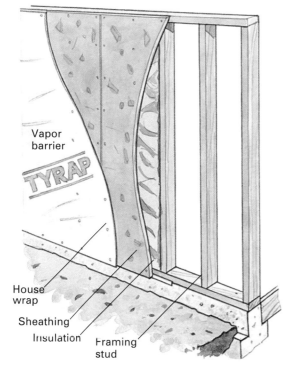

Vapor barrier

TYRAP

House wrap

Sheathing

Insulation   Framing stud

To sheath the walls, install sheets vertically and leave a gap of about ⅛ inch between them. Overlap the house foundation by 1 inch. Nail the sheets directly to the studs with 1½-inch (4d) galvanized nails spaced 12 inches apart.

Trying to add a lot of insulation to a home when re-siding can create problems at windows and doors. However, adding house wrap and ¼-inch fanfold insulation will make your home more energy efficient without much trouble. Because this combination cuts down on air infiltration, most people feel it makes the house seem warmer than its R-2 rating would suggest.

First install the house wrap. This material is designed to allow moisture out but keep air from coming in. Cut it to fit around windows and staple it to the sheathing. Seal seams at the doors and windows or where the wrap overlaps, using special house-wrap tape.

House wraps can be applied over asphalt-impregnated roofing felt that was once commonly laid over sheathing. If your home was built in the mid 1970s and is wrapped with sheets of plastic, however, remove them. The plastic traps moisture in the walls where it can create rot.

Staple fanfold insulation over the house wrap with ½-inch long staples. Then put a few 1-inch roofing nails in every 2 feet along the edges to keep it from blowing off. Don't seal the joints with tape.

LEVELING AND MEASURING TOOLS

Most homes are not plumb and square. Installing siding with perfectly horizontal lines when the building is tilted will accentuate the slant of the windows and doors and magnify the problem visually. It's best to follow the tilt of the building so the finished project will look normal.

The best way to make your siding look right is to work either from the top of the foundation or the bottom of the soffits. Check several windows and doors, the top of the foundation, and the bottom of the soffit in several places with a 4-foot level. If most of the windows or the doors seem to follow either the soffit or foundation, use that one as your reference point. If all seems equal, use the soffit, which is the easiest to gauge on.

It's also important to make sure the bottom course of siding meets evenly at the corners of the home. For this reason, it's best to start at one corner—the lowest one—and work around the home in both directions.

A fluid level works around corners and over obstructions

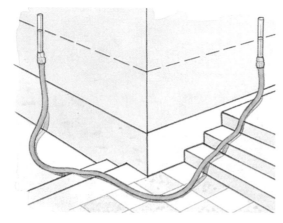

A fluid level, which works over long distances and around corners, can help you can determine whether all the corners of your home are level. It works around corners, but not over obstacles that are higher than the points you're trying to measure. Go around those obstacles. If your home is close to level, you shouldn't have trouble putting the siding on straight.

THE STORY POLE

A story pole helps you determine spacing for shingle and horizontal wood siding. This homemade jig also helps keep courses straight for vinyl and metal siding.

Make the story pole from a straight 1×4 that is long enough to reach from the top of the wall to a point below the bottom of the sheathing. Stand the pole against the wall next to a window. Mark the pole at the bottom of the sheathing, the bottom of the windowsill, and the top of the window drip cap.

Measure the distance from the bottom of the sheathing to the top of the wall. Divide that distance by the maximum siding exposure (from the siding instructions), and round up to determine the number of siding courses. For instance, if the distance is 8 feet and the maximum exposure for the 12-inch siding is 11 inches, you will need nine courses of siding. ([8×12]/11=8.727, which rounds up to 9.) Because another piece won't overlap the top course, subtract the overlap (1 inch) from 8 feet, then divide by 9 pieces. ({[8×12]-1}/9=10.55.) The result is very close to 10⁹⁄₁₆ inches, which is the ideal exposure. From these measurements, figure out where most of the windows will fit. If this measurement means that siding will have to be cut to leave narrow strips at the top or bottom, adjust your measurement. This may even mean adding another piece of siding.

When you determine the proper exposure, measure and mark on the story pole where each piece will start. Use a square to draw a line across the pole so you can use it from either edge.

You can't change the exposure for vinyl or metal siding. However, vinyl and metal sidings are sold in different styles and heights and one may work better than another on your home. Also, these hollow sidings—especially vinyl—can be stretched or shortened by pulling too much or too little. Mark the story pole with the normal exposure, and use it to keep the courses straight and level.

Another homemade jig that helps keep siding straight is an exposure jig. Cut pieces of scrap plywood to the height of the exposure. Gauge from the bottom edge of an installed course and to the next course with them.

INSTALLING FURRING

In some cases, you'll need to add furring strips to the wall to provide an adequate nailing surface. Installation of shingles over nonplywood sheathing would be an example. Furring strips are inexpensive 1×3s nailed into the studs, so you can drive the shingle nails into solid wood for a better hold. The story pole will help you figure out where to place the strips. Put shim shingles behind the furring strips as necessary to keep the surface level.

You'll also need furring strips when installing siding over existing clapboard or shingles. Nail on vertical furring over the old siding where it's over the studs to make the wall flat. Install furring around windows and doors to provide a level nailing base.

A story pole helps you plan where siding will meet doors, windows, and the soffit. You can also use it to keep siding courses straight.

Furring strips provide a flat surface over an irregular one (shown) or provide a nailing base for some siding, such as shingles.

DOORS AND WINDOWS

Details will take up a large amount of your time with most siding jobs. Most of the details involve windows and doors. Trim and accessories made for vinyl siding can simplify the detailwork when installing any kind of siding.

NEW WINDOWS?

If you've thought about installing new windows or doors, consider replacing them before you put on new siding. Replacing them later might require removing and replacing parts of the new siding. New windows are also available with different jamb widths. You can avoid adding jamb extenders to old windows by ordering jambs wide enough to fit a wall made thicker by new siding.

Window replacement can be a big project. If both window replacement and new siding are on your list, do the windows first.

INSTALLING JAMB EXTENDERS

When you install new siding over old, the added thickness often means that the window jambs (or frames) are no longer flush with the siding. You can correct this by applying jamb extenders around the doors and windows before re-siding.

To make jamb extenders, rip knot-free (clear) 1× lumber to a width equal to the thickness of the new siding. Cut the pieces on a table saw to keep the edges straight.

Then, for either a door or a window, carefully pry off the exterior casing (trim) and set it aside for reuse. Trim the top jamb extender to the correct length, and nail it to the edge of the top jamb. Next, butt the two side extenders up underneath the top piece. Trim the bottoms of the side extenders to match the angle of the sill and nail them in place. Countersink the nails with a nail set and fill the holes with exterior-grade wood putty. Replace the casing—using new exterior grade casing (not finishing) nails—after the siding has been installed.

When window jambs must be extended, sometimes the sills must also be extended. If the sill is round nosed, plane it flat. Rip a length of sill extender from stock the same thickness as the existing sill and nail it in place. Set the nails and putty the holes. Fill any gap between the extender and sill with putty and sand when dry. Finally, repaint the jamb extenders and sill.

INSTALLING FLASHING

Flashing keeps moisture from getting behind wood-framed doors and windows. Metal-framed and vinyl windows normally don't require flashing because their nailing flanges act as flashing. Preformed metal Z-flashing is available in standard sizes. Nail the flashing to the sheathing above the door or window with one edge of the flashing hanging down over the window casing.

METAL AND VINYL WINDOWS

Shim metal and vinyl windows outward to meet the new siding. Start by removing the exterior window casing. Then cut and remove the siding all around the window to expose the nailing flanges that hold the window in place. The flanges are about 1 inch wide, so measure 1½ inches out from all sides of the window and snap chalk lines. Set the blade on your circular saw ⅛ inch deeper than the thickness of the siding and cut along the lines. Save the siding pieces to use for shims when you replace the window. Pull the nails from the flange with a claw hammer or prybar, then remove the window.

Drill holes in the siding pieces to avoid splitting them, then nail them back in place around the window opening. Place the window back in the opening, check that it is level, then plumb and nail it in place through the flanges. New siding will be brought to the edge of the window and the casing will be put back to cover the gap between the new siding and the window. You may have to install jamb extenders inside the home.

ALUMINUM WRAP

Instead of painting old wooden window casings and jambs, many professionals wrap them in factory-finished aluminum. This provides a permanent finish and can cover many kinds of cosmetic problems, including marred wood and chipped paint. To do this yourself, you'll need to rent a brake—a viselike tool that makes sharp bends in sheet metal. You'll also need a supply of utility knife blades and a pair of aviation snips.

The idea is to create a three-side C-channel of aluminum stock that can be nailed over the old parts of the windows. Start at the bottom of the window and measure the width of the sill. Then measure out from where the windowpane begins to the edge of the sill, as well as the thickness and any distance below the sill that returns to the siding. Using a straightedge and a utility knife (you'll have to make several passes), cut a piece of aluminum to the right size. Put the long piece of aluminum into the brake so that it will crease the aluminum at the point where the sill turns downward. Instead of estimating angles, just make it a right-angle crease and adjust the angle when you install it. Then, turn the piece of aluminum around and crease it where the sill begins to return back to the house. When you're done, you should have a piece that, with a little adjustment, covers the sill.

You're bound to make mistakes, but don't worry; prefinished aluminum is inexpensive.

Work your way up each side so that each layer above delivers water onto the piece below so the water can't get behind the aluminum. If you have angled casings, try a few scrap pieces to see what works best. For the top piece, add an extra inch and an extra bend so the wrap can serve as the flashing. Make your normal two bends with the extra inch for the topside. Then turn the wrap upside down and crease it at the 1-inch mark so this flange will run up the wall. When completed, caulk the joints.

VINYL WINDOW AND DOOR TRIM

Even if you're siding with something other than vinyl, trim and accessories made for vinyl siding can be useful.

Vinyl window and door trim quickly replaces regular casing on new windows or on metal and vinyl windows that have been re-hung. It is simply nailed to the sheathing next to the window, much like vinyl J-channel molding. (See page 73.) The siding slips into a channel on the outside edge. Thick sidings won't fit into this groove. If using something firmer than vinyl siding, make sure it doesn't distort the vinyl window trim.

This vinyl molding can replace the wooden casing of older windows. You will still have to extend window or door jambs if they don't protrude beyond the new siding, but this work might not need to be as precise. For instance, if you are reusing the wooden casing, the jamb extenders need to precisely fill the gap created by the additional layer of siding. With the vinyl window and door trim, you can extend the jamb out further and then surround the frame (created by the jamb extenders) with the vinyl window trim.

CAULKING

Caulk around windows and doors before installing vinyl or aluminum siding. With wood siding, caulk windows and doors after installing the siding.

If you leave the existing siding, metal and vinyl windows will have to be remounted farther out. They are attached to the house with flanges beneath the siding. To remove them, start by prying off the trim.

To reach the flanges, cut around the window as deep as the siding and about 1½ inches away from the edge. Remove the pieces of siding but don't discard them. Pull the nails in the flange, and remove the window. After removing the window, nail the siding pieces back into place.

Nail through the flanges to remount the window on top of the siding you just reinstalled. The new siding will fit against the window frame.

INSTALLING PANEL SIDING

lywood and hardboard panel sidings are great for do-it-yourself jobs because they're inexpensive and easy to install.

CHOOSING THE PANELS

Standard panel sizes are 4×8, 4×9, and 4×10 feet. For new installation, buy siding at least ⅜-inch thick for plain panels, or ½-inch thick if patterned or grooved. When re-siding over an irregular surface, such as clapboards, use panels that are ½ inch or ⅝ inch thick.

INSTALLING THE PANELS

Locate the wall studs first. To find studs, look for edges and nails in the old siding. If the siding has been removed, you may be able to see nail holes in the sheathing. An electronic stud finder works well, too. Snap a vertical chalk line down the center of each stud.

Panel siding is awkward and requires a lot of nailing, so get help. One person can hold a panel in place while the other nails it.

Place panels vertically, with the edges centered on studs. Proper positioning of the first panel is critical, because all successive panels must fit against it. If the first one is out of line, the others will be.

Let the bottom edge of the panel overlap the foundation wall by at least 1½ inches, but keep it at least 8 inches above the ground. Nail panels ½ inch thick or less with 2-inch (6d) rust-resistant nails and ones more than ½ inch with 2½-inch (8d) nails. Space nails 6 inches apart around the edges and 12 inches apart into the studs between the edges.

Install overlapping panels so that each succeeding panel laps over the previous panel's rabbeted edge. This way, you can drive nails into the overlapped edge to nail both panels securely.

Leave ⅛ inch between panels. To space plain-edge panels, tap in a 3½-inch (16d) nail alongside the edge of the panel at the top and bottom. Remove the spacer nails as you nail the next panel in place.

Cut plywood and hardboard panels with a circular saw, with the panel's exposed face down to minimize splintering. Mark cutting lines on front, then transfer them to the back.

Siding with panels requires cutting the sheets to fit around windows and doors. Install a Z-flashing where panels meet vertically to keep water out.

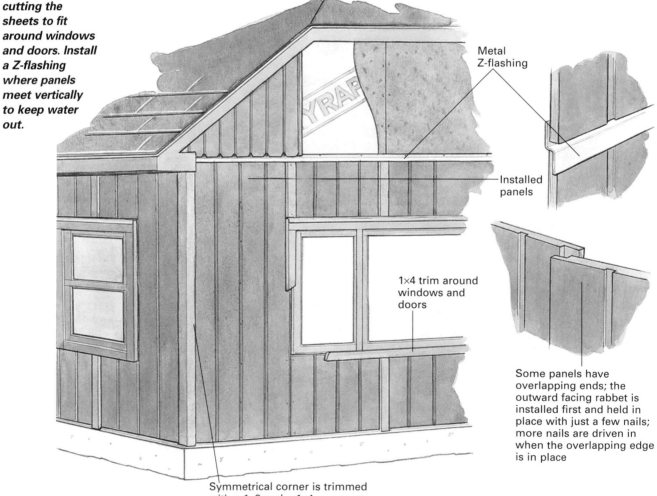

Metal Z-flashing

Installed panels

1×4 trim around windows and doors

Some panels have overlapping ends; the outward facing rabbet is installed first and held in place with just a few nails; more nails are driven in when the overlapping edge is in place

Symmetrical corner is trimmed with a 1×3 and a 1×4

CUTTING AROUND OPENINGS

Cut full sheets to fit around openings when possible; this reduces the number of seams around doors and windows, producing a better appearance. Both edges of all panels must be nailed into studs; this can sometimes be difficult when going around windows and doors because studs aren't always in uniform locations above doors and above and below windows. An electronic stud finder is almost a necessity for this. You may need to rip a 4-foot-wide panel narrower to center each edge on a stud.

Carefully measure for any cutout to avoid expensive mistakes. Take your measurements from the mating edge of the previous panel and from a reference line that matches either the top or bottom of the panel, depending on which is more convenient. Make the opening ¼ inch larger on each side, the top, and the bottom to make fitting the panel around an opening easier.

From your measurements, lay out the cutting line on the panel with a pencil. If you're working on the face, don't press so hard you make grooves, but draw the lines dark enough to follow.

When the opening falls at the edge of a panel, you can make the top and bottom cuts straight in from the panel edge. But the other side will require a pocket cut. To make one, place the circular saw at one end of the line, with the front of the saw's sole plate resting on the panel. Pivot the saw up to raise the blade above the panel. Then, with the blade poised over the line, raise the saw's blade guard, start the saw, and lower the blade into the wood until the sole plate rests on the panel. Then cut along the line, and shut off the saw. Do not back up the saw. Instead, finish the cut with a handsaw.

Cut smaller or oddly shaped holes with a portable jigsaw. Bore holes for pipes with a portable drill and holesaw. Bore the hole ¼ inch larger than the diameter of the pipe. When you can't slide a hole in a panel over a pipe, cut out a strip from the hole to the bottom or edge of the panel that is the same width as the diameter of the hole. Slide the siding in place over the pipe, then glue the strip back into the slot. Caulk around the pipe.

GABLE ENDS

When installing panels on the gable ends of a house, first cover the top edge of the main course of panels on the end of the house with Z-shaped flashing. The bottom edge of the flashing laps over the top of the siding and the top edge fits behind the gable-end siding.

To calculate the gable-end cuts, measure the distance from the top of the plywood at the corner to the bottom of the rafter or soffit, then subtract ¼ inch for clearance. Measure 4 feet along the end of the house. Use a 4-foot level to determine the point exactly above this horizontal measurement, then measure up to the bottom of the rafter and subtract ¼ inch. Pencil these measurements on a sheet of siding. Then connect these measurements—which will be the line of the roof—with a straight edge, and cut.

After the gable-end siding is up, caulk the gap between the tops of the panels and the rafter and cover the joint with trim boards.

TRIMWORK

Caulk the gap between the panels and the window or door jamb, and between panels meeting at the corners.

Trim outside corners with a 1×3 on one side and a 1×4 for the overlapping piece. You can do the same with inside corners, or you can nail in a length of cove molding, as shown above, or a 1×1.

Trim windows and doors with 1×4s, as illustrated. Butt joints rather than mitered corners at the top minimize water running underneath. The top piece usually overlaps the sides. Where the panels meet the rafters or soffits, cover the tops with 1×2s. Caulk all trim edges.

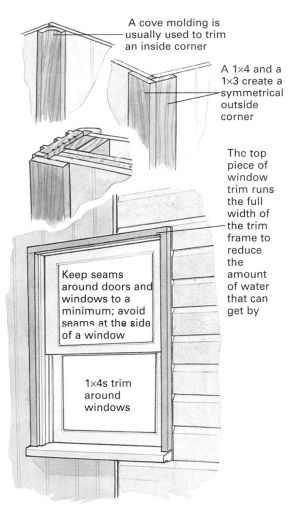

A cove molding is usually used to trim an inside corner

A 1×4 and a 1×3 create a symmetrical outside corner

The top piece of window trim runs the full width of the trim frame to reduce the amount of water that can get by

Keep seams around doors and windows to a minimum; avoid seams at the side of a window

1×4s trim around windows

FIBER CEMENT PANELS

These procedures for panel siding apply to fiber cement panels, too. Cut the panels with masonry blades, following the siding manufacturer's recommendations. To avoid cracking the panels, predrill nail holes.

VERTICAL WOOD SIDING

Vertical siding boards, usually ¾ inch thick, range in width from 3½ to 11¼ inches. Redwood and cedar are popular for vertical siding. Pine and fir can also be used if painted or stained.

TYPES OF BOARDS

Some siding boards, such as channel siding, have rabbeted edges for a weathertight fit. In another common style called board-and-batten, 1×2 or 1×3 boards called battens are nailed over the joints between wider siding boards. Shiplap and tongue-and-groove boards, more commonly installed as horizontal siding, are sometimes put on as vertical siding.

PREPARING THE WALL

To apply vertical siding over an irregular surface, put on horizontal furring strips at 16- or 24-inch intervals. Sometimes, 2×4 blocks placed between the studs at 24-inch height intervals provide nailing surfaces.

Nail the furring into wall studs. To locate the studs, look for exposed nails in the old siding. If the siding has been removed, look for nail holes in the sheathing to locate the studs. An inexpensive electronic stud finder is an easy way to locate them. Snap a vertical chalk line down the center of each stud.

Vertical wood siding, which runs the same direction as the framing lumber, requires furring strips on irregular surfaces for nailing.

Install flashings around wood-framed doors and windows before you install the siding (see page 64).

INSTALLING THE SIDING

Start installing the siding at the lowest corner of the building. Plumb the first board with a level; keep it vertical even if the building is out of plumb. You can hide out-of-square deviations with trim at the corners after you finish the siding.

When applying tongue-and-groove siding, start with the grooved edge along the corner of the building. Tap succeeding boards into place with a hammer, protecting the tongue edge with a scrap piece of wood. You can either face-nail the boards or, for narrower boards, blind-nail them by starting a nail at the tongue and angling it back.

For board-and-batten, leave a ¼-inch gap between the boards—they can swell when damp, so they might buckle. Nail the boards first, then add the battens over the joints.

COVERING GABLE ENDS

To cover gable ends, either carry the siding all the way to the roofline in a continuous sweep, break at the top of the wall and cover the gable with a second course (install Z-flashing over the bottom course), or shingle the gable end to contrast with the siding.

Find the slope of your roof (see page 22), then find the angle of the rafters with the chart on page 23. Use this angle on a miter saw or mark the siding with a pencil and use a triangular square. Because cutting to length involves an angle, it's a little difficult. The easy way is to first decide about how long the board will be. Play it safe and add 1 inch to this length. Then make your angular cut. Measure from the tip of the angle and make a straight cut on the other end of the siding for a proper fit. This will waste a little wood and requires an extra cut, but it's a lot easier to do.

CORNER TREATMENTS

Caulk the corner before covering. The standard corner treatment for vertical siding is to overlap by the same amount that the batten is thick—a standard batten with another board that is wider.

HORIZONTAL WOOD SIDING

Clapboard siding remains a favorite among homeowners. Its straight, horizontal lines enhance the appearance of virtually any house.

PREPARING THE WALL

When re-siding, it is important to locate all the wall studs. Look for nails in the old siding or, if it's been removed, in the sheathing. An inexpensive electronic stud finder will help. Snap a vertical chalk line down the center of each stud.

When siding over old horizontal siding, nail down any warped and bulging boards. Sight along the house to spot them, and nail them back into place. If you are applying horizontal siding over an irregular surface, such as existing siding, shingles, or uneven concrete block, apply vertical furring strips first to provide a flat nailing surface.

Stand your story pole (see page 63) at each corner and transfer the marks to the house. Make additional marks on the walls at intervals shorter than the length of the siding. For instance, mark every 10 or 11 feet if you're using 12-foot siding. Check with the story pole periodically to make sure the siding doesn't wander up or down.

For beveled clapboard, install a starter board around the bottom of the house to tilt the first piece out to match successive rows. Make the starter board about 1½ inches wide and the same thickness as the top edge of the siding board. You don't need a starter board for shiplap or tongue-and-groove siding.

If doors and windows are wood framed, install flashing there before the siding.

INSTALLING THE SIDING

Align the first board with the first set of marks and nail it on. Nails should penetrate at least 1½ inches into the studs, so you'll probably use 2½-inch (8d) nails. Use nails specifically designed for siding.

Blind-nail tongue-and-groove siding that's up to 6 inches wide with finishing nails, as shown at right. On beveled and shiplap siding and tongue-and-groove siding wider than 6 inches, nail straight into the stud—called face nailing. Install cedar or redwood siding that won't be painted with aluminum or stainless-steel nails. Galvanized nails will make rust stains on the siding.

Ensure that the courses run straight by checking the story pole markings. Siding with formed edges, like shiplap, fits together, but it's still important to check the courses.

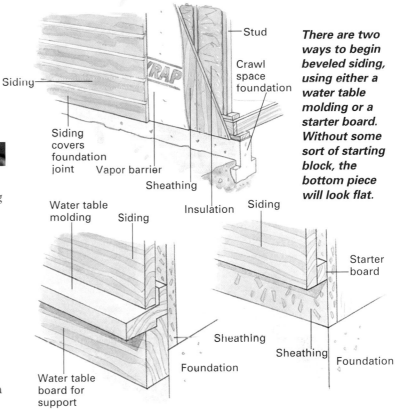

Siding
Siding covers foundation joint
Vapor barrier
Sheathing
Stud
Crawl space foundation
Water table molding
Siding
Insulation
Siding
Water table board for support
Sheathing
Foundation
Starter board
Sheathing
Foundation

There are two ways to begin beveled siding, using either a water table molding or a starter board. Without some sort of starting block, the bottom piece will look flat.

The story pole is crucial when installing beveled siding. It's the surest way to keep each board straight and the exposures even.

A common, and expensive, problem when nailing solid wood siding is splitting the siding at the end of each piece. The best way to avoid this is to predrill the nail holes with a bit smaller than the nail. Blunting the nail point can reduce splitting too—the blunted nail tears its way through the wood instead of splitting it like a wedge. Blunt a nail quickly by holding it with its head on a solid surface and striking the point with a hammer.

GABLE ENDS

To cut the boards at an angle matching the roof slope at the gable ends, determine what the slope is. (See page 22.) Use the chart to determine the angle. Use a triangular square to draw that angle on the siding and cut. You can cut left and right angles, then cut the piece to length by taking a section out of the middle. That way, you avoid cutting the siding to length while also cutting the angle.

Instead of carrying the horizontal pattern all the way up the gable, many people prefer to cover the gable ends with vertical siding. In this case, a Z-flashing is placed over the top edge of the horizontal siding and the vertical siding is installed over it.

BLIND NAILING PATTERN

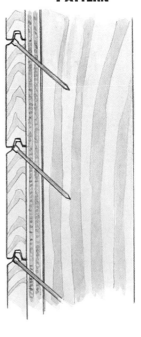

VINYL OR METAL SIDING

Together, vinyl and metal siding are by far the most popular. They've improved markedly in recent years, overcoming their earlier negative image as a cheap substitute for quality siding. These sidings are durable and attractive, come in a number of styles, and require little or no maintenance once installed. A wide range of trim pieces and other accessories—so many that one company now refers to their product line as "vinyl carpentry"—makes installation quick and easy for the do-it-yourselfer.

CHOOSING THE SIDING

Metal and vinyl sidings are available in varying thicknesses; as a general rule, thicker material is better. You'll find several quality (and price) grades on the market. Compare the features carefully to pick the right one for you. Insulated backer boards are available for many sidings—they add rigidity to the otherwise flimsy strips.

Metal and vinyl sidings usually come in strips that resemble multiple rows of traditional siding. Style names—such as triple 4 inch, double 5 inch, or double Dutch lap—refer to the appearance. Wider siding may come just one course per piece, such as single 8 inch.

Metal and vinyl siding require accessories that keep the siding in place, channel water outward, and cover the hollow ends (see the illustration on the opposite page). Many of these are referred to by the way they look in section, such as J-channel or F-channel. Other pieces are referred to by the job they do, such as starter strips, undersill trim and inside corner posts. The more complex your home's exterior, the more of these parts you'll probably need. A simple ranch-style house may only need J-channel and outside corner posts. To figure out how many of the various accessories you'll need, study the rest of this chapter to learn which parts are used in various situations, then measure the appropriate areas and order the correct amount, plus a little extra.

TOOLS AND OTHER EQUIPMENT

In addition to the regular tools needed to install siding (hammer, saw, square, chalk line, level, and tape measure), you will need some special tools and a worktable. Vinyl and metal are too flexible and too prone to kinking to lay across sawhorses for cutting. When working with vinyl siding, you'll also need tools made just for installing vinyl: a snap-lock punch, a nail-hole punch, and an unlocking tool.

Vinyl and aluminum siding are relatively easy to cut, using any of three methods. For straight cuts, the quickest way is with a radial-arm or circular saw fitted with a fine-tooth blade (40 to 60 teeth) installed backwards. Wear safety glasses and ear protectors for

TOOLS FOR VINYL AND METAL SIDING

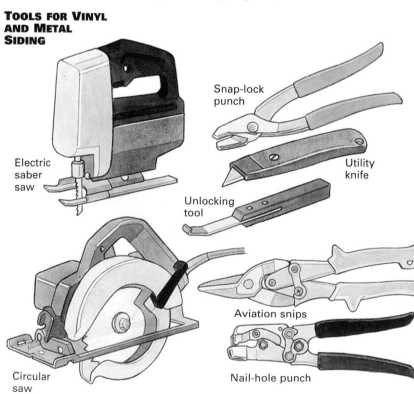

Electric saber saw

Snap-lock punch

Utility knife

Unlocking tool

Aviation snips

Circular saw

Nail-hole punch

LOCK IN A QUALITY JOB

The strength of metal and vinyl siding lies in the way the strips lock together. Many siding problems come from incomplete or improper locking. When you install one piece above another, you need to lift it up enough to snap the two pieces together. The best way to do this is to catch the bottom edge of the upper piece with your fingertips with your palms against the siding. Then lift up to lock the upper piece to the lower one. To check it, press downward on the upper piece. If the joint slides apart easily—and silently—it isn't locked.

Proper nailing of vinyl and metal siding allows for expansion. Drive nails in straight, in the middle of a slot, and leave a 1/16-inch gap between the nailhead and the siding.

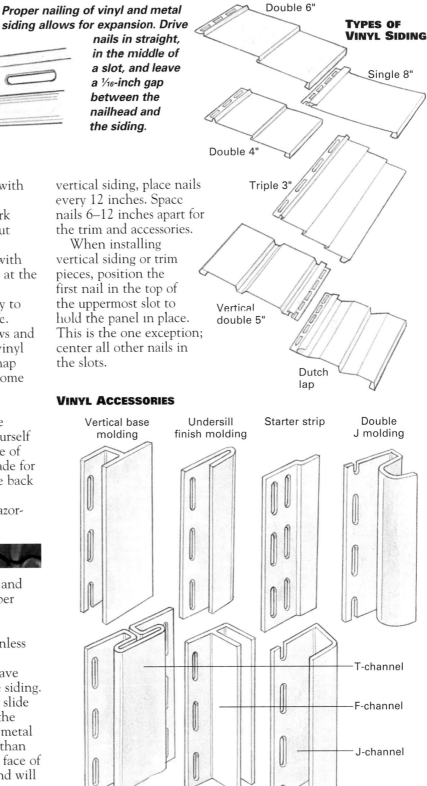

TYPES OF VINYL SIDING

Double 6"

Single 8"

Double 4"

Triple 3"

Vertical double 5"

Dutch lap

cutting. Do not cut any other material with the saw blade installed backwards.

Aviation snips (compound snips) work well, too. Snips leave a rougher edge, but J-channel or other pieces of siding will generally hide them. For a cleaner cut with snips, don't close the blades completely at the end of each stroke.

The third way to make a cut is simply to make multiple passes with a utility knife. This method works well around windows and doors. Pros often cut a deep groove in vinyl siding with a vinyl scoring tool, then snap the siding apart. This technique takes some practice to master.

Cutting steel siding is much more difficult—one of the main reasons some manufacturers don't sell to the do-it-yourself market. Aviation snips can handle some of the cutting; a portable jigsaw with a blade for thin steel will do the rest. Saw from the back for best results.

Cut steel and aluminum siding has razor-sharp edges. Always wear gloves.

NAILING PROCEDURE

Vinyl and metal siding panels contract and expand with temperature changes. Proper nailing will allow for this movement.

Here are the two main rules:
■ Center the nails in the panel slots unless otherwise specified.
■ Do not drive in nails completely. Leave 1/16 inch between the nail head and the siding.

Nailing this way allows the siding to slide freely as it expands and contracts. For the same reason, any nail through vinyl or metal siding should go through a hole bigger than the nail shank. Never nail through the face of the siding or the nail head will show and will cause the strip to buckle.

Drive nails in straight and level to prevent the head from distorting and buckling the nailing flange. If you use a pneumatic stapler or nailer, get a vinyl siding attachment to ensure correct installation of the fastener.

For horizontal siding, drive nails into the wall studs—ideally every 16 inches. In high-wind areas, put nails every 8 inches. For vertical siding, place nails every 12 inches. Space nails 6–12 inches apart for the trim and accessories.

When installing vertical siding or trim pieces, position the first nail in the top of the uppermost slot to hold the panel in place. This is the one exception; center all other nails in the slots.

VINYL ACCESSORIES

Vertical base molding

Undersill finish molding

Starter strip

Double J molding

T-channel

F-channel

J-channel

Outside corner post

Inside corner post

VINYL OR METAL SIDING
continued

Vinyl siding snaps together for strength. The bottoms of new courses lock into the tops of existing courses.

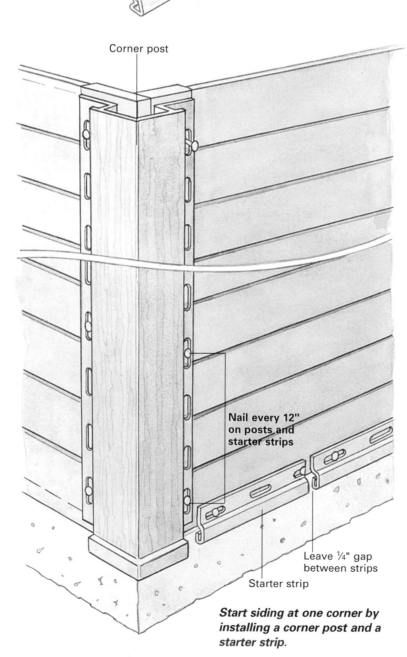

Corner post

Nail every 12" on posts and starter strips

Leave ¼" gap between strips

Starter strip

Start siding at one corner by installing a corner post and a starter strip.

INSTALLING STARTER STRIPS AND CORNER POSTS

Start installing horizontal siding by attaching corner posts and starter strips. Find the lowest point of the home where the siding will start. Transfer this lowest point measurement to all corners of the house and snap chalk lines all around the house to position the starter strips.

VINYL SIDING: Install the corner post first at the lowest point, reaching up to where the soffit is or will be. The corner posts can warp in storage, so work slowly from the top down, using a level to keep it straight. Nail alternate sides as you work down. If the wall height exceeds the length of the corner post, cut a second section to overlap the top of the lower post by 1 inch.

Install starter strip around the bottom of the house, starting ¼ inch from the corner post. Manufacturers' recommendations for starter-strip location in relation to the bottom of the wall vary; always check the instructions with your siding. Leave a ¼-inch gap between starter strips. If the siding starts lower than an obstacle such as a flight of steps, run J-channel around the obstacle as though it were a window (see Dealing with Doors and Windows on the opposite page).

METAL SIDING: Install the starter strip around the bottom of the house, starting ¼ inch from the corner of the house, unless the siding manufacturer provides a different dimension. Check the siding instructions for the proper placement of the starter strip in relation to the bottom of the wall. Metal siding begins at the edge of the house. Corner pieces are installed later to cover this edge.

INSTALLING HORIZONTAL SIDING

Lock the first strip of siding into the lip of the starter strip. If working with vinyl, slide the siding into the corner post, leaving ¼ inch for expansion. Nail the strip at 16-inch intervals or into the studs. Overlap subsequent vinyl strips in the same course 1 inch at the factory-notched ends. Overlap from front of the house to back so that the joints will not be as visible. Do not nail closer than 6 inches to any joint. Vinyl siding will stretch; do not pull the strips tight as you nail.

Slide the cut ends of strips into corner posts or J-channels whenever possible to allow factory edges to meet. If the factory edges don't meet, lay the factory end over the cut end. Some manufacturers suggest cutting 1½ inches off the nailing flange of the cut end when overlapping.

Metal siding won't overlap like vinyl does, so one strip joins to another with a specially made trim piece. If you're using 8-inch noninsulated metal siding, backer tabs can be inserted behind the joints to add rigidity.

Install the first course all around the house, then start the second course. Vinyl and metal siding strips lock together, strengthening the siding. Before nailing a strip, make sure it has locked firmly into the one below. Stagger joints as you go up a wall so they don't all end at the same place. An easy way to do this is to start at one corner and work across the wall. The end cut from the last piece of siding in a course then becomes the starting piece for the next course.

DEALING WITH DOORS AND WINDOWS

It's best to trim doors and windows as you approach them instead of before you start. Here's why: The bottom of the window can take one of two different types of trim, depending on where the siding meets the underside of the window. Usually, you will install undersill trim, sometimes spaced out from the wall by lath or scrapwood. However, if the siding meets the underside of the window where the siding bends out to begin another layer of siding, you may have to use a J-channel. You probably won't know this until you get there.

When the siding gets to the window, find out which molding you will need. Cut a length of the molding equal to the outside width of the window, then nail it on.

Although the bottom edge can change, J-channel always goes along the sides and top.

THE EASY WAY: Cut the side lengths exactly as long as the window frame and nail them into place. Cut the top J-channel long enough to span from the outside edge of one side J-channel to the outside edge of the opposite one. Before installing it, use the aviation snips to cut each end of the channel back the width of the J-channel, forming tabs (shown at right). Nail the top piece of J-channel flush with the top of the window frame. Bend down the tabs, then drill them

and nail them to the side of the window frame. This will act as flashing over the side members.

THE NEATER WAY: This method is similar, but you miter the top outside corners to better frame the window. Cut the sidepieces longer than the window frame by the thickness of the J-channel. Then cut and remove the channel portion until it's flush with the top of the window frame. Prepare the top piece as in the previous method, but before installing it, cut the two ends to a 45-degree angle at the corners. Then install it the same way as in the previous method.

Finally, caulk the gap where the J-channel and undersill meet the window frame to prevent water from getting behind them.

INSTALLING WINDOW TRIM

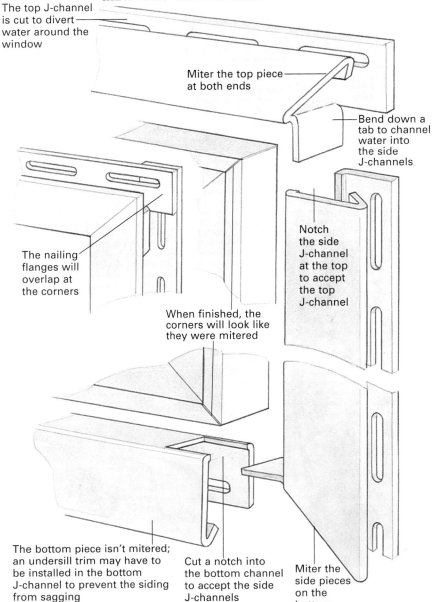

The top J-channel is cut to divert water around the window

Miter the top piece at both ends

Bend down a tab to channel water into the side J-channels

The nailing flanges will overlap at the corners

Notch the side J-channel at the top to accept the top J-channel

When finished, the corners will look like they were mitered

The bottom piece isn't mitered; an undersill trim may have to be installed in the bottom J-channel to prevent the siding from sagging

Cut a notch into the bottom channel to accept the side J-channels

Miter the side pieces on the bottom

VINYL OR METAL SIDING
continued

SIDING BELOW A WINDOW: You will probably have to cut siding to fit around the bottom of a window. The easiest way to do this is to snap a scrap of siding into the course below the window on each side and slide their ends into the J-channels on the window sides. Measure between the ends of the scrap pieces to find the width of the window. Then measure the distance from inside the J-channel to either the corner post or the edge of the next piece of siding.

On a worktable, transfer these measurements to the piece of siding that will go around the window. Remember to allow

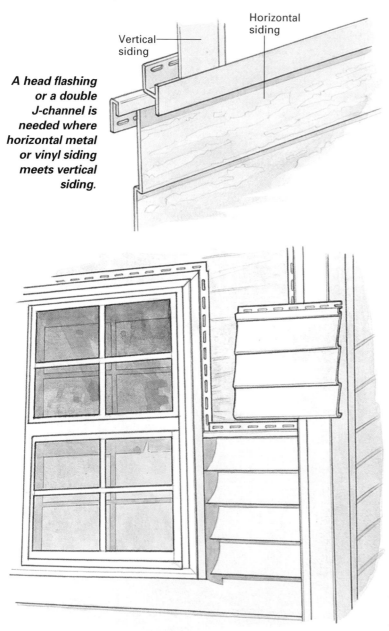

Vertical siding

Horizontal siding

A head flashing or a double J-channel is needed where horizontal metal or vinyl siding meets vertical siding.

Don't stretch short pieces; they have to remain evenly spaced so the top piece will fit properly.

¼ inch clearance at each side of the window and the corner piece. For vinyl siding, allow a 1-inch overlap with other pieces of siding. Metal siding will have a connector piece and no overlap.

Use tin snips for vertical cuts; use a utility knife or scoring tool for scoring horizontal cuts, then snap out the section. If panels have an insulation backing, cut the insulation before scoring the panels. Use a saber saw for steel siding.

Test-fit it by bringing the piece up from below and fitting it into all the trim pieces. When metal siding fits, it usually can be installed. For vinyl siding, form a series of raised lugs—one every 6 inches—with the snap-lock tool before installing the piece. These lugs will snap into the undersill molding to prevent the siding from sagging under the window. Some aluminum siding require lugs, too.

SIDING AT THE TOP OF THE WALL:
When you reach the soffit, nail a strip of undersill trim just under it. Measure the distance between the top course and the trim strip and cut the panels to fit. Using the snap-lock punch, indent the upper edge of each panel at 6-inch intervals (as described above for under windows) so that the raised lugs are on the outside. Lock the last piece into the lip of the panel under it and push the top of the panel into the trim strip. The raised lugs will catch and hold the panel in the trim strip.

If you need to remove a piece of vinyl siding after it has been installed, use the unlocking tool. Jam the tool into the locking strip of the panel above the one you want to remove. Apply a firm downward pressure on the tool and slide it the length of the panel. This will free the top panel enough so that you can reach underneath it and remove the nails holding the panel you want to remove. It's difficult to remove a piece of metal siding once it's installed.

INSTALLING VERTICAL SIDING

Determine the lowest point of the house, which is where the siding will start. Transfer this lowest point measurement to all corners of the house and snap chalk lines all around the house. Install special vertical base molding or J-channel at the bottom edges, locating it as specified in the siding manufacturer's instructions. When joining two lengths of vertical base flashing, trim off the nailing flange about 1 inch, then overlap the pieces. At the top of the wall, install inverted J-channel. For vinyl siding, install corner posts as explained on page 72.

PUTTING UP THE SIDING: Start in the middle and work outward with vinyl siding. For metal siding, start at one side and work to the other. Either way, first drop a plumb line to mark the edge of the first strip. Align the strip exactly on the plumb line, leaving a ¼-inch gap at the top and bottom for expansion. Drive in the first nail in the top of the uppermost slot to hold the strip in position, then nail it every 6 to 12 inches.

Cut the remaining panels to fit between the base and trim strips and nail them through the flanges every 6 to 12 inches.

If the height of the house requires additional courses, install another piece of vertical base molding at the top of the first course. Begin the second course with a ¼-inch gap at the flashing.

Install J-channel on the sides of windows and doors and an inverted J-channel under a window. On top of the window or door, nail on a special window/door cap first, then install J-channel. Measure, mark, and cut the siding to fit around windows and doors as explained on the opposite page.

When vinyl siding ends in a corner post, nail a length of undersill trim in the corner post's channel. Fur the trim out to the front of the channel.

Cut the siding to fit, then form lugs every 6 inches along the edge with the snap-lock tool. The undersill trim will grip these lugs to secure the siding.

GABLE ENDS

To cover a gable end with vertical siding over horizontal siding, install inverted J-channel underneath the rake of the roof. Run vertical base molding across the top of the horizontal siding. For vinyl siding, install starter strip, splitting the triangular area into two smaller triangles, as shown in the illustration at right. Determine the angle of the roof and cut a scrap of trim to that angle as a test piece. When the angle is correct, the scrap of siding will serve as a template for cutting the strips. Install the strips, working from each starter strip outward. Cut the angle at the top of each strip, using the template. Trim each strip to length with a straight cut across the bottom.

When installing metal siding in a gable end where it starts at a point, pound in a nail—with the head sticking out about ⅛inch—to start the piece. Glue this edge with construction adhesive, too.

METAL-SIDING CORNERS

For steel and aluminum siding, the last step is to install metal corner covers. There are two kinds—one snaps on, the other nails on. Follow the manufacturer's guidelines for the one you use, and take time to make sure they're straight.

WASH IT UP

When you're finished, wash the siding with a mild soapy water to remove fingerprints or other dirt, then rinse with water. Oil from skin can be burned into the siding by the sun.

There are two types of corner posts for vinyl siding. One type is made from a single piece of vinyl. The other has a snap-on cover.

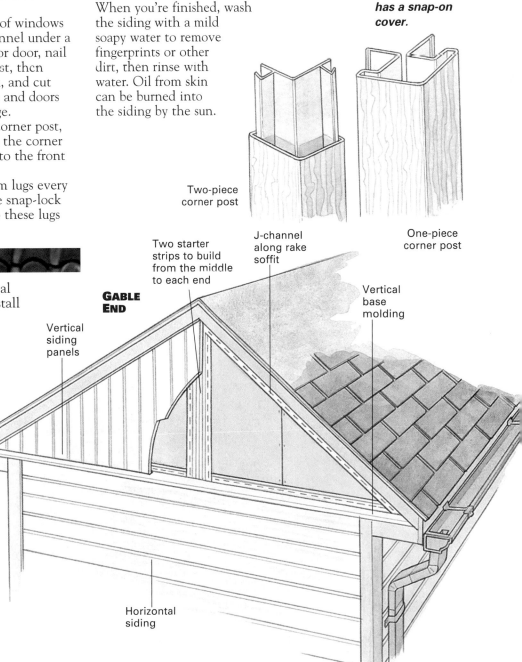

Two-piece corner post

J-channel along rake soffit

One-piece corner post

There are two types of corner posts for vinyl siding.

Two starter strips to build from the middle to each end

Vertical base molding

GABLE END

Vertical siding panels

Horizontal siding

SHINGLE SIDING

Cedar shingles have several advantages over other siding: They last a long time, require no painting, and can be installed single-handedly. Although shingles are more expensive initially than other types of siding, their maintenance costs will be low. They also are attractive when used with other siding for gable ends. The rules here apply to shakes, too.

PREPARING THE WALL

Shingles are normally applied over solid plywood or oriented strand board wall sheathing, old plywood siding, or horizontal furring strips. Don't apply shingles to reconstituted wood sheathing—the soft material that's like a bulletin board. It's important to use a modern house wrap that allows the shingles to breathe while still blocking wind infiltration. Red building paper is adequate, but if your home is wrapped with black asphalt paper or polyethylene, replace it with house wrap.

Cut and fit special metal flashing over all door and window casings before shingles are applied. This flashing is like Z-bar flashing used for panel siding, but should extend 4 to 6 inches up the wall. If you can't find this flashing, either make it or use Z-bar flashing and then flash the Z-bar with strips of 6-inch galvanized metal. If the windows and doors need paint, do this before the shingles go on.

After the wall has been prepared, check the shingle exposure with the story pole. The idea is to have shingle butts in line with the bottom of the windowsill and the top of the drip cap, if possible, to minimize cutting shingles to fit.

SHINGLING THE WALL

Double-up the first shingle course across the bottom. To keep this course level, put a shingle at each corner of the building with the butt 1 inch below the sheathing. Tack a small nail at the butt edge of these shingles and stretch line between them. Align all intervening shingles on this line.

You can snap chalk lines or tack a straight 1×4 across the shingles of all successive courses in line with the story pole marks and align the shingle butts on it.

If you are shingling a house that is not level, let the first course follow the slant of the house rather than running it level. Adjust each successive course by $\frac{1}{8}$ inch until level. This slight change will not be noticeable.

Fasten shingles with galvanized ring-shank nails to keep them from working loose. This is particularly important when nailing shingles to $\frac{3}{8}$-inch plywood siding. Each shingle is nailed up with two nails, regardless of its width. Place the nails 1 inch above the butt line for the next course, and $\frac{3}{4}$ inch in from the edges.

Kiln-dried shingles should be spaced about $\frac{1}{8}$ inch apart to allow for expansion. However, many shingles are being sold green, or freshly cut, and will shrink as they dry, so check with your dealer. No gap between shingles should be closer than $1\frac{1}{2}$ inches to a gap in the course below. And no gap should be in line with one less than three courses below. When putting a course above a door or window, don't let a gap line up with the edge of a window or door.

Where shingles must be cut to fit around obstructions, measure and cut with a handsaw or a coping saw. For fine trimming when fitting along window or door casing or trim boards, try to use whole shingles with straight edges and fit smaller shingles elsewhere in the course to make them fit.

If shingles must be shortened to fit above a window or door opening, trim the shingles from the butt end. Trimming along the top will leave thicker shingles under the row above, causing a bulge.

CORNER TREATMENTS: Where shingles meet at corners, they can be bevel-cut, woven, or butted against trim.

Mitering is the most painstaking method. Each shingle must be fitted against another, and the edges bevel-cut with a power saw. Although bevel-cut corners are good-looking, they are the least effective at blocking wind-driven rain. The corners can eventually develop gaps, too.

Woven corners provide better weather protection and are more commonly used. Shingles for this corner treatment also must be individually fitted and cut.

To weave corners, you alternate shingles on the two meeting sides so the shingles on one side butt up against those on the other side. To start, nail the bottom layer of the doubled starter course around the bottom of the house. Then start the next layer of shingles. The illustration of the woven corner shows how the top shingle on side A extends beyond the corner. Put the side B shingle against the extended shingle and trace its outline along the back of the side A shingle. Cut along that line, and nail the shingles in place.

On the next row up, repeat the process, this time extending the end shingle on side B beyond the corner and, on its back, marking the outline of the shingle on side A. Continue up the wall in this manner.

Corner trim boards offer the most effective weather protection and easiest way to shingle corners. Use one 1×4 and one 1×3, with the wider board overlapping the narrower one's edge. Cedar or redwood are best. Simply lay the shingles up against the boards; only straight trimming will be involved.

Inside corners can be woven, or you can butt the shingle edges against a 2×2 set into the corner. Run a bead of caulk between the shingles and corner boards.

Trim the shingles in the final course to fit. Crown the last course with a 1×4 or a molding to cover the crack at the soffit.

WOOD SHINGLE SIDING

- Molding
- Shingle
- Sheathing
- 2×2 inside corner block
- Mitered inside corner shingle
- Shingle butted against corner block
- Double starter course of shingles
- Starter strip
- Water table
- Water table board
- Double starter course of shingles
- Side B
- Side A
- Alternate sides overlapping
- Sheathing
- 1×4s
- Shingles
- ¾" quarter round

WOVEN CORNER

OTHER MATERIALS

Combinations of materials often produce first-rate results, as in this traditional wood and stucco half-timbering. You could create a similar look with a stucco substitute and boards.

Real stucco, brick, and stone are durable and beautiful. If this is what you want, leave installation to a pro—if for no other reason than the sheer tonnage of the materials involved. The work involves special techniques and equipment, too. However, there are modern alternatives that a do-it-yourselfer can apply in small quantities to complement other siding.

HARMONIZE

One of the biggest problems people have with the way their newly sided home looks is that it's generally too much of a good thing. Pale yellow siding from foundation to soffit on all four walls often announces that this was a do-it-yourself re-siding job.

One way to combat this is to follow the lead of professional architects by installing multiple siding products on homes, especially on the front. Hardly a 1950s rambler or 1960s ranch-style home was built without a half-brick front or a stuccoed area around a picture window.

You can also enhance otherwise unnoticeable features of your home. If your home was built with a plain concrete block or plywood-sided chimney, a stone or brick veneer can make it look much better.

Most stone and brick veneers are expensive, but are affordable when used sparingly. Premixed stucco alternatives are practically the cheapest product available and go on easily.

SOME OTHER IDEAS

Here are some ways to incorporate other looks into your home's facade.
■ Apply brick or stone veneer on the lower half of the front of the home, topped with vertical siding or half-sheets of panel siding.
■ Stucco or brick-veneer the area around the front door where people get closest to the house.
■ Stucco an area around the home's largest front feature, such as a picture window.
■ Garages are prominent on many homes; put brick veneer on the narrow walls next to the garage door.

■ Install brick veneer below all the windows on the front of the house to give the impression they're sitting on solid brick.

■ Apply a piece of rough-sawn cedar on top of the first-story siding on the gable end of a home. Add three more pieces of cedar in a W pattern above it and apply stucco substitute in between the boards for a half-timber look.

PREPARATION

Most of the products of this type are unique to their manufacturer so these are general guidelines.

It's vital to install all stucco substitutes and stone and brick veneers over properly prepared surfaces. The best surface would be cementitious backer board. This is a ½-inch panel of reinforced concrete that any mortar or adhesive adheres to easily. To install it, drill holes for special screws and then fill gaps with a special compound. Once in place it should last for 30 years or more. Don't extend the cementitious board beyond the area where you will be applying stucco, stone, or brick because it is difficult to nail through it to attach other types of siding.

You could apply stucco substitutes directly over old masonry surfaces such as concrete block or stucco. To properly prepare the surface, you may need to wire-brush or sandblast to remove dirt, loose masonry, and paint. Many of the products will go over primed exterior plywood or oriented strand board (OSB). Some manufacturers insist you use their brand of primer. Unless the manufacturer advises so, don't use hardboard or reconstituted wood sheathing as a backer board.

Brick and stone veneers might require that metal lath, or chicken wire, be nailed to the surface with rubber-washered nails.

Cover any adjoining wood, metal, or vinyl trim with wide masking tape. Stucco is messy, whether the real stuff or the new substitutes. Cover bushes and wear old clothes.

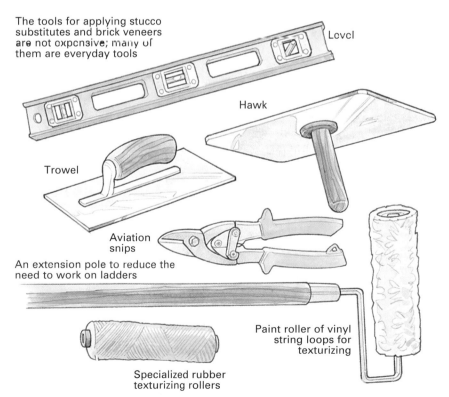

Manufactured stone veneer looks like masonry but installs like wall tile. Stone is often applied as an accent with other siding.

TOOLS FOR APPLYING STUCCO ALTERNATIVES AND BRICK VENEERS

The tools for applying stucco substitutes and brick veneers are not expensive; many of them are everyday tools

Level

Hawk

Trowel

Aviation snips

An extension pole to reduce the need to work on ladders

Specialized rubber texturizing rollers

Paint roller of vinyl string loops for texturizing

OTHER MATERIALS

continued

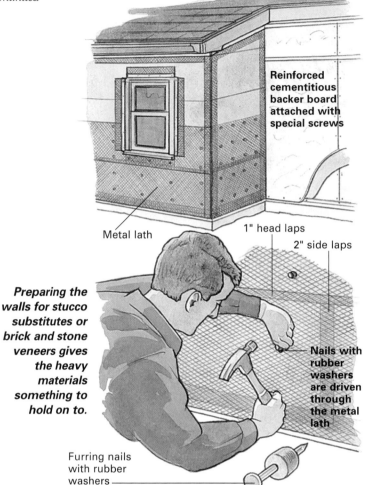

Reinforced cementitious backer board attached with special screws

Metal lath

1" head laps

2" side laps

Preparing the walls for stucco substitutes or brick and stone veneers gives the heavy materials something to hold on to.

Nails with rubber washers are driven through the metal lath

Furring nails with rubber washers

APPLYING STUCCO SUBSTITUTE

Applying stucco substitute to a wall is straightforward. However, you may need a little practice to get the finish just right. Apply some on a piece of scrap plywood first and experiment with the finishing techniques before applying it to your home.

One brand of stucco substitute will create a pattern by simply troweling over it. The design is "programmed" into the product, and the manufacturer offers a variety of textures. With other stucco substitutes, you create the finished pattern. This gives you complete control over it, but each finish takes time to master.

The easiest way to finish stucco substitute is to go over it with a texturizing roller cover, which fits an ordinary paint roller. The roller cover has loops of plastic string that catch the soft stucco compound and lift it to create a stippled pattern.

Another method is using a wet trowel to knock down some of the stippling made by the roller to give it an old-world, hand-applied look.

To apply the stucco, begin in a corner. Use the trowel to lift some of the stuccoing compound out of the bucket, then put it on a hawk. A hawk is a large square of aluminum with a handle. Hold the hawk against the

Texture is created with a roller

Stucco substitute is troweled on

Cementitious backer board

A typical stucco substitute is troweled onto the cementitious backer board by pushing it off the hawk, which is held next to the wall. Then a texturizer is rolled over the surface.

wall and push some of the compound onto the wall. Use the trowel to work the compound back and forth a few times to get it to adhere to the backer board, as shown in the illustration on the opposite page. Put on enough compound to cover about 9 square feet.

At that point, stop applying compound and go over the material with the texturizing roller to create the stipples. Don't work the edges of the fresh area too much—it will dry too quickly. (You'll finish working the edges when you apply the next batch of stucco.) Try to complete a whole wall or large area in one session.

If you can't complete a wall, roll the texture to the edge of the stucco, then feather those edges with the roller to make them a little thinner than the main area. When you start again, you can apply more soft stucco compound over the edge and work in a texture.

Unlike real stucco, most of the substitutes look best when painted with primer and two topcoats.

BRICK AND STONE VENEERS

Installation of most brick and stone veneer is similar to tiling: You set the brick or stone pieces into mortar applied over a solid base. Spaces between the pieces are usually grouted, but some materials don't require it.

Symmetrical stones and brick are easier to install because there is less cutting and less time is spent trying to get the pieces to fit together.

A water-cooled, diamond-tipped saw is the best tool for cutting brick and stone. (You can rent a wet saw from tile dealers or rental stores.) If you're just cutting a few pieces, buy an inexpensive masonry blade that fits a circular saw.

When installing brick and stone veneer, always follow the material manufacturer's instructions for specific installation information.

If you're working with irregularly shaped stones, work out the layout on your lawn first so you don't have to

reposition stones in mortar. Start at the bottom of one corner and begin by applying the mortar to an area that's 3 feet by 3 feet. Special corner pieces are available for brick and some cast stones. Set the stones or bricks into the mortar. On smaller stones or in difficult places, the mortar can be applied to the back of the stone first with a putty knife (called back buttering). Tap the stones into place with a wooden or rubber mallet.

When the stones or bricks are all set, wait for the mortar to dry—usually two days. If the product requires grouting, squeeze mortar into the gap between stones with a grout bag, which looks like a cake decorator's bag.

When you're done, coat the stone or brick and the grout with a special sealer so water won't be absorbed into them.

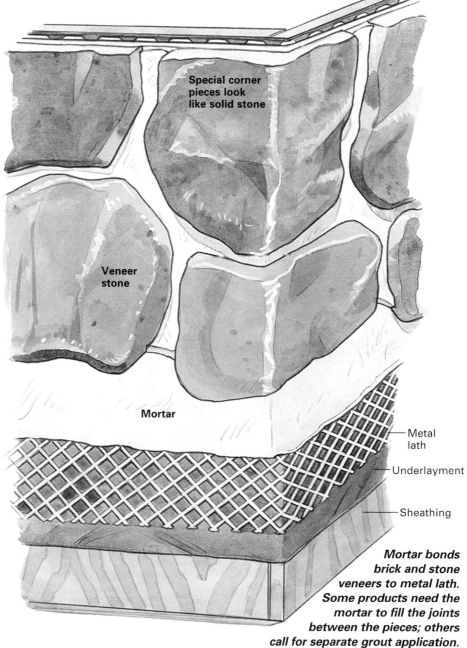

Special corner pieces look like solid stone

Veneer stone

Mortar

Metal lath

Underlayment

Sheathing

Mortar bonds brick and stone veneers to metal lath. Some products need the mortar to fill the joints between the pieces; others call for separate grout application.

SOFFITS AND FASCIA

Aluminum or vinyl soffit and fascia are popular even on homes sided with other materials. The reason is simple: The fascia (the vertical board at the eaves) and the soffit (the horizontal panel between the eaves and the wall) are difficult to paint and maintain. Low-maintenance aluminum and vinyl reduce home-care chores.

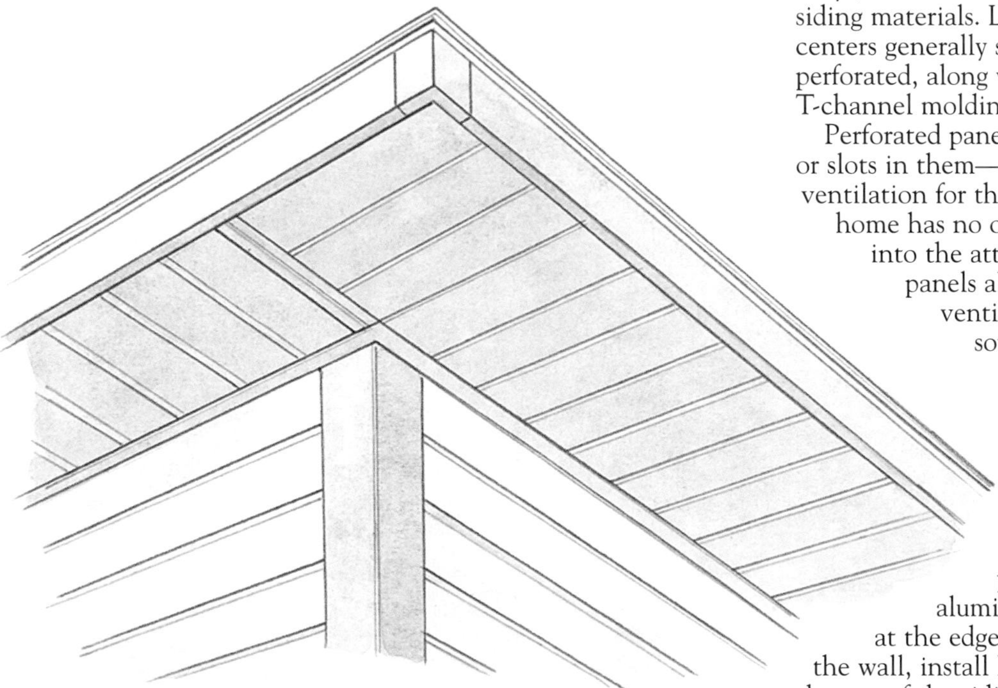

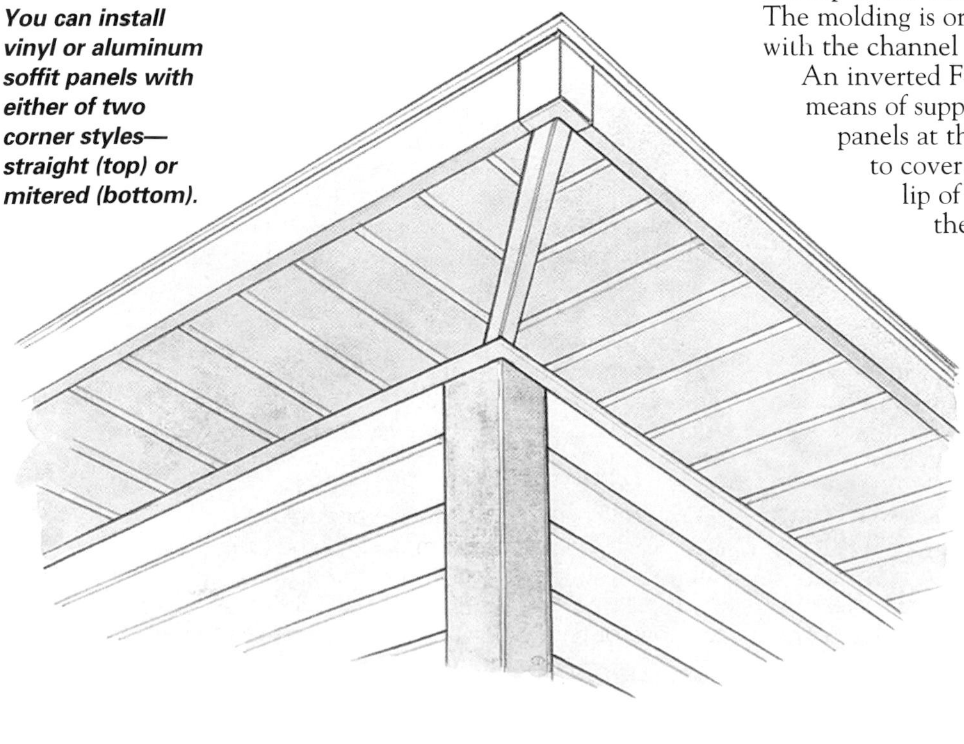

SOFFITS

Soffits differ greatly from house to house, depending on the overhang of the eaves. Some eaves extend out from the house 4 feet; others are just inches long. Because of this, siding materials to cover soffits are manufactured as long panels that can be cut to the length needed to run from the house to the edge of the eave.

Panels for soffits, available in aluminum or vinyl, are unlike either horizontal or vertical siding materials. Lumberyards and home centers generally sell two types—solid and perforated, along with the F-channel and T-channel moldings for installation.

Perforated panels—they may have holes or slots in them—are designed to provide ventilation for the attic (see page 53). If your home has no other openings to allow air into the attic, however, the perforated panels alone won't solve attic-ventilation problems. If the soffits you're replacing have ventilating openings cut in them, you probably need to install perforated soffit panels.

INSTALLING SOFFIT PANELS:

Solid and ventilated panels of either vinyl or aluminum lock together at the edges to form a solid cover. At the wall, install F-channel moldings along the top of the siding to support the panels. The molding is ordinarily installed inverted—with the channel opening toward the bottom. An inverted F-channel is also the best means of supporting the outer end of the panels at the eaves if you don't intend to cover the fascia boards. Nail the lip of the channel to the face of the fascia board. As an alternative, you can hold up the panels with L-shaped vinyl or an aluminum fascia cover.

When you install the panels with two F-channels, cut the soffit panels to fit between them (allowing ¼ inch for expansion), insert the panels in the channels, and snap them together. If you decide to support the panel ends with the

You can install vinyl or aluminum soffit panels with either of two corner styles— straight (top) or mitered (bottom).

fascia cover, drill a hole through the panel and drive a nail through it into the underside of the fascia board to hold the panel in place until you install the fascia cover.

The distance from the edge of the eaves to the house can change over a run, so measure every other piece. The job goes more quickly if one person measures and installs the panels while another cuts the panels to length and hands them up. Cut aluminum or vinyl soffit material with a circular saw with a fine-toothed, carbide-tipped blade mounted backwards.

A channel is used at the corners where two dissimilar edges meet. You can use a commercial T-channel or a double track made by attaching two J-channels back to back and fastened at the bottom of a 2×2 strip nailed between the wall and fascia. It allows one run of soffit panels to fill the corner gap, while the other run ends at the channel. You can install the channel diagonally between the corner of the home and the inside corner of the fascia. However, this will require more cutting to make the final strips fit.

A T-channel is also used where the two soffits meet and at the underside of the peak of the roof.

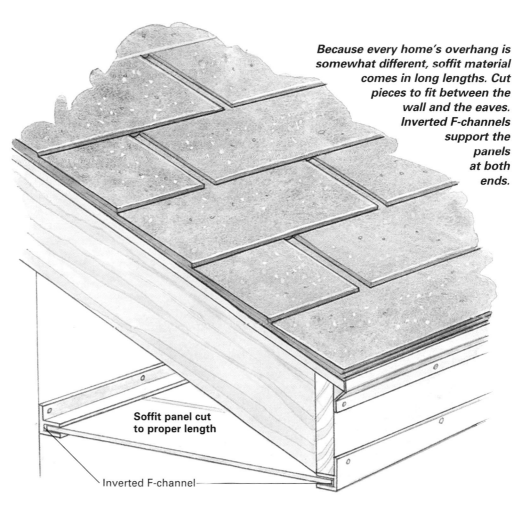

Because every home's overhang is somewhat different, soffit material comes in long lengths. Cut pieces to fit between the wall and the eaves. Inverted F-channels support the panels at both ends.

Soffit panel cut to proper length

Inverted F-channel

FASCIA

Vinyl or aluminum fascia covers complete the job. If your roof has aluminum or vinyl drip edge, cut the aluminum or vinyl fascia covering to the correct width. Slide the edge up under the bottom flange of the drip edge, then nail down the drip edge along with the fascia cover.

To install vinyl fascia where there is no drip edge, nail strips of vinyl undersill trim along the top of the fascia board, flush with the roofline. Cut the fascia cover to the required width. Form lugs every 6 inches on the fascia cover's outer face, then hook the fascia cover's lip over the bottom of the F-channel or nailed-in-place soffits and insert the top edge into the undersill trim. The lugs will lock the cover into the trim.

To install aluminum fascia covers on a house without a drip edge, it's best to cut the fascia long enough to fit tightly under the shingles that extend past the roof edge.

Fascia boards are often wavy along the length of the eaves—sometimes wavy enough that it's hard to put on aluminum fascia without creating bulges and wrinkles. You can avoid this problem by installing shorter pieces of aluminum soffit covers. Overlap the joints 1 inch or so, and caulk the joints with a matching caulk.

The fascia can be bent around corners. This gives the edges a smooth look and eliminates a common insect entry point. To turn a corner with either vinyl or aluminum, use a utility knife to score the vertical centerline of the corner on the back of the fascia cover. At the bottom of this score, cut out a 90-degree (45 degrees each way from the score line) section of the bottom L-flange to allow for bending.

REPAIRS AND MAINTENANCE

Sealing down loose shingles is a simple maintenance chore that will extend the life of your roof.

Wherever you live, the roof and siding of your house are under year-round assault from wind, rain, sun, and possibly ice, hail, or snow. Your best defense against this relentless attack is a good maintenance program.

This chapter will show you how to inspect and care for roofing, siding, gutters, and downspouts. With this knowledge, you can spot problems and correct them before they turn into major repairs or replacements.

CARING FOR YOUR ROOF

Because your house is familiar to you, you may not watch it with a critical eye. You should go on a walking tour every year to look for problems. Stand across the street

and in the backyard for a good overall look at your roof. Pay special attention to the ridge and rakes, where roofing material blows off first, and the gutters, where leaks often occur. Climb onto the roof and check the flashing around the vents and the chimney. All types of shingles can be repaired without much effort.

SHINGLES

Because shingles are small, self-contained units, you can localize the problem area without involving the rest of the roof. Most fixes require only a few spare shingles, a handful of nails, some roofing cement, and a tube of caulk.

COMPOSITION SHINGLES: If a shingle is torn or curled, gently raise the shingle, spread some cement underneath it, then press it firmly back into place. Do the same for a shingle that has been blown out of position; hold it in place with two roofing nails. Cover the nail heads with spots of caulk. If the shingle is cracked, fill the crack with caulk. Repair them in warm weather when the shingles are pliable.

Missing, damaged, or severely torn shingles must be replaced. Slide the straight end of a pry bar under the shingle to be removed and pry up the nails. Be careful when lifting the good shingle above the damaged one. In cool weather, the good shingle might break. In cold weather, the best way to remove a shingle is to slip a hacksaw blade under the shingle to be removed, cut each nail, then pull the shingle out. To replace the shingle, carefully raise the one above, slide the new one in place and nail. Put roofing cement under the edges of the new shingle and the one above to seal the repaired area.

Never attempt to replace just one tab of a torn shingle; always replace the entire shingle. However, you can make an effective (although less attractive) patch by slipping a piece of metal under the damaged shingle. Aluminum flashing—available in rolls at hardware stores—works well here. Slip the metal under the damaged shingle, then nail it in place. Cover the metal with roofing cement and press the shingle into it. Cover the problem tab with a matching caulk as an extra precaution. The patch will not be very noticeable from the ground.

WOOD SHAKES AND SHINGLES: There must be spaces between shakes and shingles so they can expand when wet, but a split shingle may let water through the roof. Small cracks in wood shingles or shakes can be filled with caulk. For a crack more than ½ inch wide, slide a piece of aluminum flashing material under the shingle. Put one nail on each side of the crack to hold the flashing, then coat the nail heads and fill the gap with a clear or matching caulk.

A fairly common problem with wood shingles and shakes is bowing. Bowed shingles or shakes should be repaired because rain can blow into the gaps. To fix a bowed shake or shingle, split it from the butt end with a wood chisel. Remove a ⅛-inch to ¼-inch sliver along the split. Nail the shingle down with one nail on each side of the split. Cover the split and the nailheads with matching or clear caulk.

Remove badly cracked or rotted wood shingles and shakes. Because all wood shingles should be nailed in place with two nails—each about an inch in from the edge—split it with a chisel at these points. It will probably split where the nail has already weakened it. Pull out the pieces. With a hacksaw blade, cut the nails that held the old shingle. Trim a new shingle or shake to size and tap it into place, remembering to allow a ¼-inch clearance on each side. Nail it with two nails right at the butt edge of the shingle above it. Angle them so when they are driven into

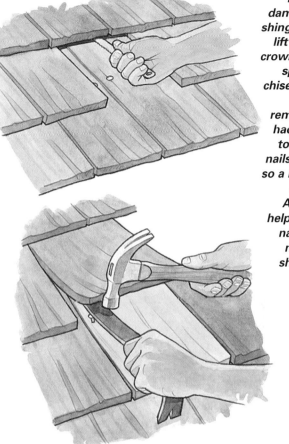

To remove a damaged wood shingle or shake, lift it up with a crowbar or try to split it with a chisel. When the shingle is removed, use a hacksaw blade to saw off the nails that held it so a new shingle can slide in. A flat pry bar helps when you nail down the new shingle, shown at left.

place, most of the nailheads will be covered. Cover any exposed nailheads with clear or matching caulk.

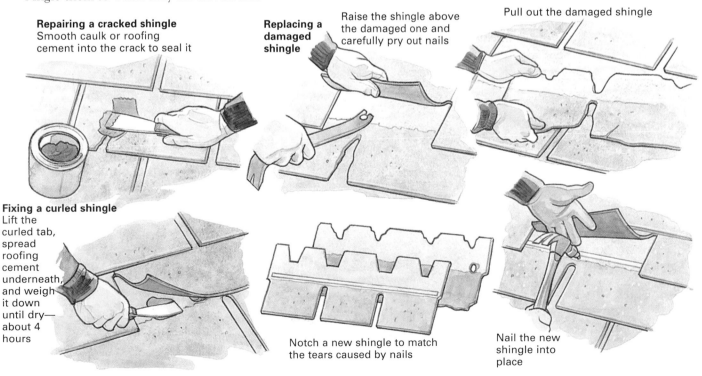

Repairing a cracked shingle
Smooth caulk or roofing cement into the crack to seal it

Replacing a damaged shingle
Raise the shingle above the damaged one and carefully pry out nails

Pull out the damaged shingle

Fixing a curled shingle
Lift the curled tab, spread roofing cement underneath, and weigh it down until dry—about 4 hours

Notch a new shingle to match the tears caused by nails

Nail the new shingle into place

CARING FOR YOUR ROOF
continued

REPAIRING A BUILT-UP ROOF

Cut out an area around the damaged area and fill it with roofing cement

Cut a patch that is larger

Nail the patch into place

Cover it with roofing cement and replace the ballast

TAR AND GRAVEL

Flat roofs are often made of layers of heavy underlayment and tar covered with fine gravel for surface protection. Leaks in these roofs, called built-up roofs, are usually difficult to spot. Two likely areas for leaks on built-up roofs are roof edges and flashing. If you suspect leaks there, coat the area liberally with roofing cement. A bubble in the roofing material could be a problem, too. But don't try to repair bubbles unless they are obviously broken or you do have a leak.

To repair a bubble, first scrape away all the gravel around the area to be repaired. Next, cut an X in the center of the bubble. Peel back each flap and liberally coat the area with roofing cement. Push the flaps back into place. Coat a square of underlayment large enough to cover the area, and nail it down with nails spaced 1 inch apart. Cover the patch and 2 inches beyond it with roofing cement, and cover the area with gravel.

A roof that leaks persistently may require a new layer or—due to its age—a total replacement. (Don't count on built-up roofs to last much more than 10–15 years.) If you decide to add another layer to the roof or replace it with another built-up roof, hire a professional crew to do a hot-mopped roof. This is hot, dangerous work; amateurs have been known to blow up the tar pot. Some cold reroofing compounds are suited to do-it-yourself application, but consider how effective this kind of repair will be.

TILE

Inspect the tile roof periodically for damaged or loose tiles. Do-it-yourself repair of tile roofs should be limited to removing and replacing broken tiles. Leave the rest to professionals.

METAL AND VINYL PANELS

Holes and cuts can be filled with a good caulk designed to adhere to the kind of panel you have. If a panel is severely damaged, you'll need to remove it and install a new one. See page 50 for instructions on installing panels.

ROLL ROOFING

Loose overlaps and tears in the roofing material frequently cause leaks. To repair a loose overlap, seal it with roofing cement, then tack it down with nails. Cover exposed nailheads with roofing cement or caulk.

Damaged roll roofing can be repaired in one of two ways: For large areas, cut out the damaged roofing the same way you would remove damaged composition shingles, then put in a new section, overlapping the ends of the original roofing. To repair smaller tears, cut a piece of roofing material large enough to cover the damage plus at least 2 inches all around it. Spread roofing cement on the back of the patch, and nail it down over the damage. Seal the edges and cover the nailheads with roofing cement.

FLASHING

If you can't find obvious damage to your roof, such as missing shingles or shakes, you can usually trace leaks to flashings or valleys.

VALLEYS: Leaks in valley flashing usually occur where water backs up in the valley due to obstructions. The water flows over the edges of the flashing and runs under the roofing material. Fix this by clearing the valley of debris, which can act like a dam to back up water.

Next, make sure that the roofing material in the valley is cut in a smooth, straight line.

If any of the material, such as underlayment or a shingle, sticks out into the valley, it can divert water out of the valley and under the shingles.

To ensure against valley leaks, carefully raise composition shingles where they meet the valley flashing and coat the area with roofing cement. Then run a bead of caulk down the valley flashing right next to the shingles. On wood shingles or shakes, just run a bead of caulk along the edges where they extend onto the valley flashing.

A break in the metal flashing itself can cause a leak. If you find a break, repair it with aluminum patching tape and roofing cement. Cut off a length of tape to amply cover the hole, peel off the backing, stick the tape in place, and cover it with roofing cement.

VENTS: Leaks occur around vent pipes when the caulk or roofing cement has shrunk or cracked. A new bead of caulk is the cure.

Inspect for damage to the roofing surface around and above the vent pipe. A crack in a shingle or tile will let water run under the metal flashing and down the vent pipe. Slightly raise the roofing material above the vent and spread roofing cement under it.

Also, see if the roofing material around the flashing is cut smoothly. If part of a composition shingle, wood shingle, or shake protrudes slightly, it may divert water under the flashing. Trim the problem shingle with aviation snips or heavy-duty shears (a knife might cut the flashing metal), then caulk.

On tile roofs, check the concrete grout (mortar) around vents. You can seal cracks temporarily with caulk, but the mortar should be chiseled out and replaced with new grout.

CHIMNEY FLASHINGS: Flashing around a chimney consists of base and cap parts (see illustration at right). Leaks frequently start where the cap flashing sets into mortar between the bricks. If there appear to be only one or two spots of loose mortar, scrape it out and fill the gap with butyl rubber caulk, which adheres well to masonry.

If the mortar is in poor condition, break it all out with a ⅜-inch cape chisel (a narrow-tipped cold chisel), and remove the cap flashing. Remove old mortar at least ½ inch deep and clean the area thoroughly with a wire brush.

New mortar doesn't bond well with old mortar. You can coat old mortar with a bonding agent, available at hardware stores. Or, you can soak old mortar and surrounding bricks with water. This prevents the old mortar from drawing too much moisture out of the new mortar, weakening it.

For the patching material, use a premixed mortar or make your own from 1 part cement and 3 parts fine sand. When the flashing has been reinstalled, coat the seams with butyl rubber caulk.

ICE DAMS

In cold climates with heavy snowfall, snow along the edge of the roof over the eaves can melt and refreeze, creating ice dams. Water from melting snow higher on the roof then pools up behind the ice dam and backs up under shingles. Good attic ventilation is the best prevention; it helps keep the roof deck cold, so the snow doesn't melt and refreeze. Another solution is to install heating cables along the roof edge. The cable, available at hardware stores, clips to the shingles in a zigzag pattern and plugs into an electrical outlet. The heat prevents ice buildup.

REPAIRING A LEAKY CHIMNEY FLASHING

Broken mortar

Step flashing

Cap flashing

Broken mortar

Cap flashing

Step flashing

Shingle

Remove old mortar with a cape chisel

Replace flashing using new mortar

CARING FOR SIDING

Look carefully at your siding material, watching for loose, split, or rotting boards or shingles. Make a list of all the potential trouble spots you see, then take steps to solve the problems.

BOARD SIDING

Splits can occur in board siding, especially in areas of extreme weather. But split boards are easy to repair or replace.

REPAIRING SPLIT BOARDS: A siding board may split near an end where it was

nailed. This should be repaired immediately to prevent rainwater from leaking behind it. Don't pull the nail where the wood is split or you'll mar the siding. Pry the split farther apart with a pry bar. Then coat the interior of the split with epoxy resin glue, which is waterproof. When the glue is tacky, push the split together again.

To prevent further splitting, drill two pilot holes smaller than the shank of a 2½-inch (8d) nail on both sides of the split over a stud. Nail the siding through these holes. Set the nails; cover with wood putty that matches the house paint.

If the split is between studs, drive shingle shims above and below the piece of siding to force the split together until the epoxy dries.

REPLACING BOARDS: If a siding board is badly splintered or rotted, it must be replaced.

■ **TONGUE-AND-GROOVE:** To remove and replace a section of tongue-and-groove siding, first locate the nearest studs on each side of the damaged area. Tongue-and-groove siding is blind-nailed, so this can be difficult. Use an electronic stud finder.

Make cuts in the board section to be removed down the center of a stud so there will be wood to nail the ends of the new and old pieces into. Mark the center of the studs and then use a circular saw to make a pocket cut on the line. Do this by raising the blade guard and resting the saw on the front of the shoe. Start the saw and lower the blade into the board. Do not cut the adjacent boards; instead, finish the cuts with a chisel. Now split the damaged board down the middle with the chisel, or cut it with the saw. Pry it out and remove any nails.

To slip the replacement board in place, first trim off the back part of the groove, as illustrated, slip the board in place, and nail it to the studs. Set the nailheads and cover with wood putty.

■ **LAPPED SIDING:** Siding such as clapboard, shiplap, and other styles of lapped siding is removed in about the same way as tongue-and-groove. Center cuts on the studs nearest each side of the damaged area. Lapped siding is easier to remove because there is no tongue locked in a groove. To avoid scuffing paint, pound wedges of wood, backed up with a rag, to pry out the board. Caulk the edges of the new piece, fit it into place, and nail.

PLYWOOD SIDING

Because of plywood's inherent strength, damage is not common. If your siding

HOW TO REPLACE A PIECE OF TONGUE-AND-GROOVE SIDING

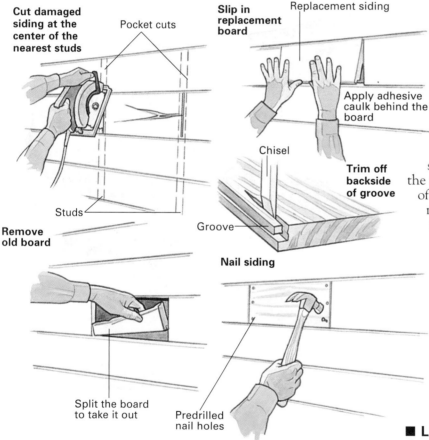

Cut damaged siding at the center of the nearest studs

Pocket cuts

Studs

Remove old board

Split the board to take it out

Predrilled nail holes

Slip in replacement board

Replacement siding

Apply adhesive caulk behind the board

Chisel

Trim off backside of groove

Groove

Nail siding

PAINT PROTECTS

Well-protected redwood or cedar siding can last more than 50 years if it's protected with paint or solid, opaque stains.

Paint doesn't just make a house look better. It's a self-sacrificing protectant. It takes the abuse of rain, sunshine, dust, and other natural elements that would otherwise harm the wood underneath. When paint flakes off, rot can set in. Keeping your home painted is the single best way to preserve your wood-sided home.

becomes damaged, however, it is usually best to replace the entire panel. A patched section will be quite noticeable. To replace a panel, remove any battens over the edges and trim around windows. Then pull the nails along the edges and take off the panel. Nail the replacement in place, then paint or stain to match the rest of the siding.

SHAKES AND WOOD SHINGLES

Repair damaged shake or wood shingle siding as you would a roof (see page 84).

STUCCO SIDING

Cracks are the most common problem in stucco siding. To fix them, gouge out the stucco in the crack with the point of a can opener. However, if it's concrete that cracked once, it will probably crack it again. The best way to repair a crack is with acrylic silicone caulk. Run a bead in the crack and—using the tip of a bristled brush—try to replicate the stucco finish. Caulk comes in several colors; try to match it. If the stucco has been painted, touch up the repaired area.

VINYL OR METAL SIDING

Fill small holes in vinyl or metal siding with a matching caulk, but replace seriously damaged pieces. Dents in aluminum siding can often be removed without replacing the panel, or can be left as is. Touch-up paint will hide scratches in the paint on metal siding.

REPLACING A VINYL PANEL: You'll need an unlocking tool to remove a damaged panel. One end of this simple device is shaped like the panel-locking strip. Insert the tool into the locking strip at the top of the panel you want to remove. Apply a firm, downward pressure on the tool and slide it the length of the panel, freeing the panel enough for you to

reach underneath and lift it up. Prop up the panel with a block of wood and remove the nails holding the damaged panel in place. After locking and nailing the replacement panel into position, relock the upper panel with the unlocking tool.

REPLACING AN ALUMINUM PANEL: Carefully cut the panel just below the piece of siding by repeatedly scoring it with a utility knife. After cutting, disengage and remove the damaged panel. Trim the nailing and locking strip from the replacement panel. Run a bead of construction adhesive along the entire length of the damaged panel underneath the panel above it.

To install the replacement panel, slip its upper edge beneath the panel above the damaged area and then lock it into the lip of the panel below. Apply firm pressure over the area of the cement bead so that it will adhere to the replacement panel. Clean off excess construction adhesive with mineral spirits.

REMOVING A DENT FROM AN ALUMINUM PANEL: Panel replacement is the best answer when you have numerous small dents, such as those resulting from a heavy hailstorm. But there's a technique that often works for a circular dent, such as one caused by a ball striking the panel. It won't work for repairing a crease.

Fit a rubber grommet over a small sheet-metal screw and thread the screw into the center of the dent. Grasp the head of the screw with a pair of pliers and pull outward until the dent pops or flattens out. Remove the screw from the panel and fill the hole with matching caulk.

PULLING A DENT FROM ALUMINUM SIDING

Sometimes a small dent caused by a ball can be popped back. Drill a small hole and screw in a sheet metal screw. Grab the screw head with a pair of pliers and pull. Use a scrap of rubber or fabric to protect the finish. Fill the hole with matching caulk.

ROLL ON A VAPOR BARRIER

When moisture inside your house—from bathing, cooking, washing dishes, and even breathing—moves through the walls, it can push the paint off. In fact, a major cause of exterior paint failure is water vapor from inside the home.

One solution is to paint the inside of all exterior walls and top-floor ceilings with a vapor-sealing paint, such as Glidden's Insul-Aid or ICI Dulux Ultra-Hide Vapor Barrier Primer-Sealer. These paints, although not as effective as fabric vapor barriers, will markedly improve paint retention. They also improve insulation and help reduce rot caused by condensation. Make sure you follow the manufacturer's application instructions.

Vinyl siding locks together. To remove a damaged piece, unlock it from the piece above with an unlocking tool.

INSTALLING GUTTERS AND DOWNSPOUTS

On a perfectly designed house, the eaves would overhang far enough to shed rainwater to where it would cause no damage. Few live in such homes, however. The rest of us rely on gutters and downspouts. Gutters are installed on eaves to collect runoff from the roof and channel it into downspouts that direct it away from the foundation of the house.

GUTTER AND DOWNSPOUT ELEMENTS

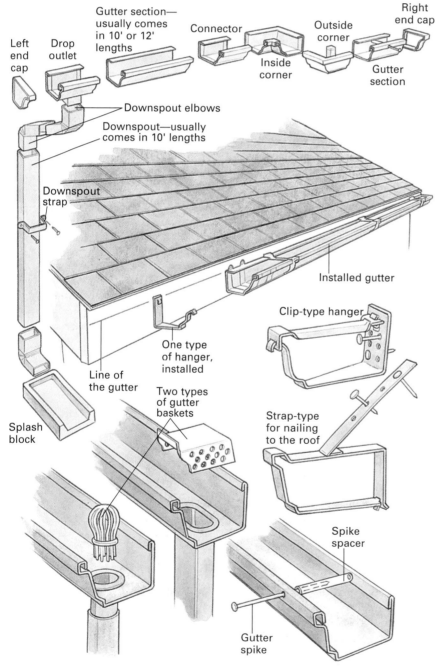

Gutter section—usually comes in 10' or 12' lengths

Connector

Outside corner

Right end cap

Left end cap

Drop outlet

Inside corner

Gutter section

Downspout elbows

Downspout—usually comes in 10' lengths

Downspout strap

Installed gutter

Clip-type hanger

One type of hanger, installed

Line of the gutter

Two types of gutter baskets

Strap-type for nailing to the roof

Splash block

Spike spacer

Gutter spike

SELECTING GUTTERS AND DOWNSPOUTS

Gutters and downspouts are commonly made from vinyl, galvanized steel, or aluminum. Unless you're working on an authentic restoration, don't use copper and wood gutters because they are expensive and difficult to install.

Vinyl and aluminum come in colors. Most lumberyards and home centers stock them in white or dark brown; any other colors are painted or special ordered. Galvanized metal gutters and downspouts are usually unpainted, so you can paint them to match your house.

Gutters and downspouts are sold in 10-foot lengths—an easy-to-handle length. Professionals install seamless aluminum gutters that are made on site by a machine that forms rolled aluminum stock into a gutter. Most gutters sold in lumberyards and home centers are 4 inches wide—adequate for most homes. A home where any roof section is larger than 800 sq. ft. (20'×40') may require a wider gutter—5 inches is the next larger size—to handle heavy runoff.

Gutter sections can be hung with any of a number of hangers, including spikes into the fascia board, brackets that mount on the fascia, and hangers that attach to the roof deck. These brackets, called strap hangers, should be installed before the roofing is put on. Downspouts are secured to the side of the house with straps or brackets.

ESTIMATING YOUR NEEDS

Measure the length of all the eaves first to calculate the number of gutter sections and supports. You only need gutters at the bottom of the roof, not along the rake. You'll need a hanger every 2 feet. Gutters also need right and left end caps, and inside and outside corners, to run the water to the spouts. A drop outlet will handle 40 feet of gutter, but usually one is installed at each corner of the house. Three elbows are needed for each drop outlet: two to bend the downspout back to the side of the house and one on the end of the downspout. Count the number of downspouts needed and add a few extra to be cut and used as connectors between the elbows at the top for longer eaves. You'll need downspout straps or brackets every 6 feet—typically three for a single-story house and four for a two-story.

You'll also need connectors to join the gutters, and screws for connecting downspout pieces. You do not need a gutter connector where the gutter sections meet at corners or drop outlets. Don't forget a splash block or downspout extension to move the water away from the house.

INSTALLING GUTTERS AND DOWNSPOUTS

Gutter brackets may attach to the roof or the fascia. Install them securely, maintaining a gutter drop of 1 inch per 20 feet.

Gutters should slope about 1 inch for every 20 feet of run. For a run of 30 feet or more, slope the gutters from the middle to a downspout at each end.

So, for a 20-foot gutter, the downspout end will be 1 inch lower than the other end. For a 40-foot run, the gutter would run from the middle to a downspout at each end, and each end would be 1 inch lower than the middle.

Where each downspout will go, measure down this amount (1 inch) from the bottom of the shingle or drip edge. Add ¼ inch for error. For our 40-foot example, it would be 1¼ inch. Pound in a nail at these spots and tie a line between them. Find the middle of the run—20 feet from either end. Measure back up the fascia the 1 inch used in our example, and drive another nail. Put the string on top of this nail. The string will now be at the top edge of the ideal gutter.

Lay out the components on the ground below the eaves. Measure the gutter runs and note the downspout locations, then cut the gutters accordingly. Cut them with a fine-tooth hacksaw. To steady the gutters while sawing, lay a length of 2×4 in the gutter about 1 inch back from the cut, then squeeze the gutter against the block.

Because of the length of gutters, two people should install them. One person can support one end while the other attaches the gutter at the other end. If you don't have a helper,

hang the far end in a loop of string tied to a nail pounded into the fascia.

Most manufacturers make a sealant for connecting gutter pieces, but some vinyl ones have built-in gaskets that make the seal.

Connect the downspout elbows to the drop outlet by drilling holes on opposite sides and inserting sheet metal screws. Connect the elbows to the downspouts in the same manner. Metal downspouts don't need a sealant. Sometimes vinyl downspouts are glued together.

For metal downspouts, bend straps to fit around the downspout and then screw them to the siding. Vinyl downspouts usually snap into U-shaped brackets that first attach to the house.

Always plan for where the water will go. Extend the downspout, landscape your yard away from the home, or build dry wells to store the water until it can be absorbed. Dry wells are usually holes about 4 feet across and 4 feet deep filled with gravel and sod on top. No one has to know they're there. Direct runoff water to a dry well, either above ground or through buried pipes.

If you have a lot of deciduous trees that drop leaves, put wire baskets into the drop hole or cover the whole gutter with an aluminum or vinyl mesh.

CARING FOR GUTTERS AND DOWNSPOUTS

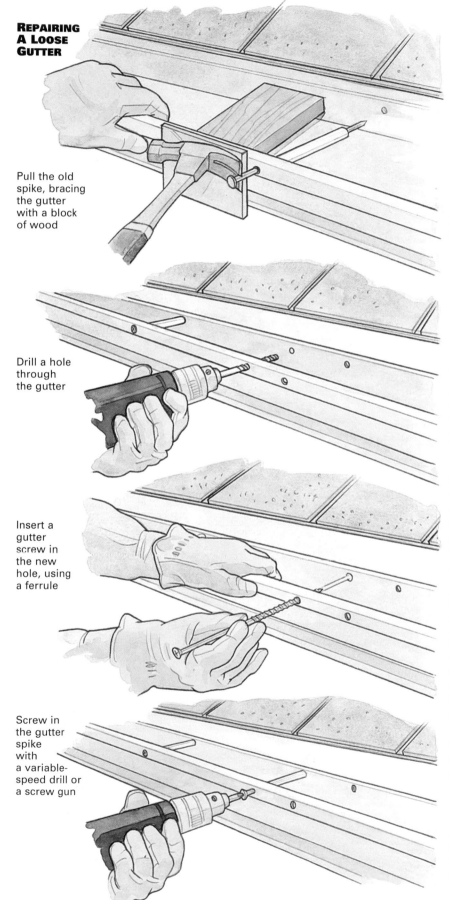

REPAIRING A LOOSE GUTTER

Pull the old spike, bracing the gutter with a block of wood

Drill a hole through the gutter

Insert a gutter screw in the new hole, using a ferrule

Screw in the gutter spike with a variable-speed drill or a screw gun

Most homes need a good gutter and downspout system to carry water away from the house. Although it is possible to build a home that doesn't need gutters, most homes rely on them to keep their foundations dry and prevent soil erosion. For a gutter system to work, it must be clean and in good repair. If your house has problems with a wet basement or crawlspace or wood rot near the foundation or fascia, inspect the gutter system.

REGULAR INSPECTIONS

A semiannual inspection of your gutters will prolong their life. Each spring and fall, clean the gutters and leaf traps of all debris. Put a hose into the downspout and make sure that the water runs freely.

Inspect your gutters from a ladder. Look for breaks in the gutters and broken support straps. Poke the wood at the eaves under the shingles with a screwdriver to see if it's still firm. Soft wood, which almost resembles paper pulp, is a sign of rot.

If there appears to be a blockage in the downspout, full water pressure from the hose may clear it. If not, run a plumber's snake, the kind used for cleaning clogged sewer lines, into the downspout. It's usually safest and easiest to do this from the ground, working upward through the downspout.

After cleaning, stand back and look closely at the gutters and downspouts. Make sure that leaf traps are in place. If you live in a cold climate, make sure that ice and snow have not distorted the drain system. Check that all the joints are still tight and there are no sags. Standing water in a gutter indicates sagging at that spot. Make sure that the gutters drop 1 inch for every 20 feet of run. Look carefully for loose nails or hanger straps on both the gutters and the downspouts.

The wood around a loose gutter spike may be rotted. Replacing the spike with a screw nearby is the best repair. Some larger-diameter screws are made to drive into the old spike hole.

COMMON REPAIRS

Here are some common gutter problems and solutions for them:

SAGGING GUTTERS:
A sagging gutter often indicates a broken or loose support. Prop the gutter into place by wedging a long pole or board under it. Inspect the hangers in the area and reattach or replace any suspect ones.

Sometimes the wood around a spike rots and the spike has nothing to hold onto. In this case, replace the spike with a screw, as shown in the illustrations on the opposite page.

HOLES IN GUTTERS: No matter what gutters are made of, they will eventually develop holes.

To repair holes in metal or vinyl gutters, first clean the area thoroughly with steel wool, working on the inside of the gutter. Small holes—the size of a nail—can be fixed with a dollop of good silicone caulk.

Cover larger holes with an adhesive-backed aluminum tape. Cover the tape with a layer of caulk or roofing cement.

Wood gutters can develop holes because of wood rot. You must wait until the wood is thoroughly dry to repair these gutters. Poke suspected areas with a screwdriver and watch for the soft wood that indicates wood rot.

Chisel out the bad wood and then soak the hole and the wood around it with a wood preservative or another product designed to dry, treat, and strengthen rotting wood. When it is dry, fill the hole with epoxy putty. Smooth it carefully until it conforms to the gutter outline. Apply a protective coat of caulk.

LEAKING JOINTS: Other problems with gutters occur at the joints. They separate because of loose hangers, ice loads, the weight of soggy leaves, and just old age. If you find a leaking joint, check for any loose hangers nearby and fix them first. On aluminum and galvanized steel gutters, use a caulking gun to squeeze silicone or butyl rubber caulk into the joint. With wood gutters, wait until the wood is completely dry, then apply butyl rubber caulk.

To repair a large hole in a metal gutter, first clean the area with steel wool. Apply a piece of aluminum tape and cover it with caulk.

Perforated vinyl panels designed to keep leaves out of the gutters slide under the first course of shingles and snap on to the outboard side of the gutter.

INDEX

METRIC CONVERSIONS

U.S. Units to Metric Equivalents			Metric Units to U.S. Equivalents		
To Convert From	Multiply By	To Get	To Convert From	Multiply By	To Get
Inches	25.4	Millimeters	Millimeters	0.0394	Inches
Inches	2.54	Centimeters	Centimeters	0.3937	Inches
Feet	30.48	Centimeters	Centimeters	0.0328	Feet
Feet	0.3048	Meters	Meters	3.2808	Feet
Yards	0.9144	Meters	Meters	1.0936	Yards
Square inches	6.4516	Square centimeters	Square centimeters	0.1550	Square inches
Square feet	0.0929	Square meters	Square meters	10.764	Square feet
Square yards	0.8361	Square meters	Square meters	1.1960	Square yards
Acres	0.4047	Hectares	Hectares	2.4711	Acres
Cubic inches	16.387	Cubic centimeters	Cubic centimeters	0.0610	Cubic inches
Cubic feet	0.0283	Cubic meters	Cubic meters	35.315	Cubic feet
Cubic feet	28.316	Liters	Liters	0.0353	Cubic feet
Cubic yards	0.7646	Cubic meters	Cubic meters	1.308	Cubic yards
Cubic yards	764.55	Liters	Liters	0.0013	Cubic yards

To convert from degrees Fahrenheit (F) to degrees Celsius (C), first subtract 32, then multiply by $\frac{5}{9}$.

To convert from degrees Celsius (C) to degrees Fahrenheit (F), multiply by $\frac{9}{5}$, then add 32.